Arrows of Freethought

G. W. Foote

Arrows of Freethought

Copyright © 2020 Bibliotech Press
All rights reserved

The present edition is a reproduction of previous publication of this classic work. Minor typographical errors may have been corrected without note, however, for an authentic reading experience the spelling, punctuation, and capitalization have been retained from the original text.

ISBN: 978-1-64799-372-6

CONTENTS

PREFACE	iv
RELIGION AND PROGRESS	1
A DEFENCE OF THOMAS PAINE	8
THE GOSPEL OF FREETHOUGHT	17
FREETHOUGHT IN CURRENT LITERATURE	25
DEAN STANLEY'S LATEST	35
GOD AND THE QUEEN	42
CARDINAL NEWMAN ON INFIDELITY	46
SUNDAY TYRANNY	49
WHO ARE THE BLASPHEMERS?	53
THE BIRTH OF CHRIST	56
THE REIGN OF CHRIST	62
THE PRIMATE ON MODERN INFIDELITY	68
BAITING A BISHOP	77
PROFESSOR FLINT ON ATHEISM	84
A HIDDEN GOD	89
GENERAL JOSHUA	97
GOING TO HELL	102
CHRISTMAS EVE IN HEAVEN	106
PROFESSOR BLACKIE ON ATHEISM	113
SALVATIONISM	122
A PIOUS SHOWMAN	126

PREFACE

I republish in this little volume a few of my numerous articles that have appeared in the Secularist, the Liberal, the National Reformer, and the Freethinker, during the last five or six years. I have included nothing (I hope) of merely ephemeral interest. Every article in this collection was at least written carefully, and with an eye to more than the exigencies of the moment. In disentombing them from the cemeteries of periodical literature, where so many of their companions lie buried, I trust I have not allowed parental love to outrun discretion.

I have not thought it necessary to indicate, in each case, the journal in which the reprinted articles were first published.

Should anyone object to the freedom of my style, or the asperity of my criticism, I would ask him to remember that Christianity still persecutes to the full extent of its power, and that a Creed which answers argument with prosecution cannot expect tender treatment in return; and I would also ask him, in the words of Ruskin, "to consider how much less harm is done in the world by ungraceful boldness than by untimely fear."

London, November 15th, 1882

RELIGION AND PROGRESS

(November, 1882)

The Archbishop of York is peculiarly qualified to speak on religion and progress. His form of thanksgiving to the God of Battles for our "victory" in Egypt marks him as a man of extraordinary intellect and character, such as common people may admire without hoping to emulate; while his position, in Archbishop Tait's necessitated absence from the scene, makes him the active head of the English Church. Let us listen to the great man.

Archbishop Thomson recently addressed "a working-men's meeting" in the Drill Hall, Sheffield. It was densely crowded by six or seven thousand people, and this fact was cited by the Archbishop as a proof that the working classes of England have not yet lost interest in the Christian faith. But we should very much like to know how it was ascertained that all, or even the major portion, of the vast audience were working-men. It is easy enough to give any meeting a name. We often hear of a Conservative Working-men's banquet, with tickets at something like a guinea each, a duke at the top of the table and a row' of lords down each side. And our experience leads us to believe that nearly all religious meetings of "working-men" are attended chiefly by the lower middle classes who go regularly to church or chapel every Sunday of their lives.

Even, however, if the whole six or seven thousand were working-men, the fact would prove little; for Sheffield contains a population of three hundred thousand, and it was not difficult for the clergy who thronged the platform to get up a big "ticket" meeting, at which a popular Archbishop was the principal speaker, and the eloquence was all to be had for nothing.

The Archbishop's lecture, or sermon, or whatever it was, contained nothing new, nor was any old idea presented in a new light. It was simply a summary of the vulgar declamations against the "carnal mind" with which we are all so familiar. Progress, said his Grace, was of two kinds, intellectual and moral. Of the former sort we had plenty, but of the latter not so much. He repudiated the notion that moral progress would naturally keep pace with intellectual progress, and he denied that righteousness could ever prevail without "some sanction from above." This was the sum and substance of his discourse, and we have no doubt that our readers have heard the same thing, in various forms of language, some hundreds of times.

Like the rest of his tribe, Archbishop Thomson went abroad for all his frightful warnings, and especially to France. He severely condemned the French "pride in progress," which led to the Revolution. His Grace has certainly a most original conception of history. Ordinary historians tell us that the Revolution was caused by hunger, bad government, and the rigidity of old institutions that could not accommodate themselves to new ideas. But whatever were the causes, look at the results. Compare the state of France before the Revolution with its condition now. The despotic monarchy is gone; the luxurious and privileged aristocracy has disappeared; and the incredibly wealthy and tyrannous Church is reduced to humbleness and poverty. But the starving masses have become the most prosperous on the face of the earth; the ignorant multitudes are well educated; the platform and the press are free; a career is open to every citizen; science, art, and literature have made immense strides; and although Paris, like every great capital, may still, as Mr. Arnold says, lack morality, there is no such flagrant vileness within her walls as the corruptions of the ancien régime; no such impudent affronting of the decencies of life as made the parc aux cerfs for ever infamous, and his Christian Majesty, Louis the Fifteenth, a worthy compeer of Tiberius; no such shameless wickedness as made the orgies of the Duke of Orleans and the Abbé Dubois match the worst saturnalia of Nero.

His Grace felt obliged to advert also to the Paris Commune, about which his information seems to be equal to his knowledge of the Revolution. He has the ignorance or audacity to declare that the Commune "destroyed a city and ravaged the land;" when, as a matter of fact, the struggle was absolutely confined to Paris, and the few buildings injured were in the line of fire. This worthy prelate thinks destruction of buildings a crime on the part of Communalists, but a virtue on the part of a Christian power; and while denouncing the partial wreck of Paris, he blesses the wholesale ruin of Alexandria.

His Grace ventures also to call the leading men of the Commune "drunken dissolute villains." The beaten party is always wicked, and perhaps Dr. Thomson will remember that Jesus Christ himself was accused of consorting with publicans and sinners. Drunken dissolute villains do not risk their lives for an idea. The men of the Commune may have been mistaken, but their motives were lofty; and Millière, falling dead on the Church steps before the Versailles bullets, with the cry of Vive l'Humanité on his lips, was as noble a hero as any crucified Galilean who questioned why his God had forsaken him.

That intellectual and moral progress naturally go together, the Archbishop calls "an absurd and insane doctrine," and he couples with these epithets the honored names of Buckle and Spencer. Now it will be well to have a clear understanding on this point. Are intellectual causes dominant or subordinate? Even so intensely religious a man as Lamennais unhesitatingly answers that they are dominant. He affirms, in his Du Passé et de l'Avenir du, Peuple, that "intellectual development has produced all other developments," and he adds:—

"It is represented that evil, as it appears in history, springs entirely from the passions. This is quite false. The passions disturb the existing order, whatever it may be, but they do not constitute it. They have not that power. It is the necessary result of the received ideas and beliefs. Thus the passions show themselves the same in all epochs, and yet, in different epochs, the established order changes, and sometimes fundamentally."

The truth is that the great moral conceptions are securely established, and the only possible improvement in them must come from the increased fineness and subtlety of our mental powers.

Civilisation and progress are, according to Archbishop Thomson, nothing but "cobwebs and terms." He besought the working men of Sheffield not to go for information to a big book written in some garret in London. His Grace, who lives in a palace at other people's expense, has a very natural dislike of any man of genius who may live in a garret at his own. What has the place in which a book is written to do with its value? "Don Quixote" and the "Pilgrim's Progress" were written in gaol; and for all Archbishop Thomson knows to the contrary every gospel and epistle of the New Testament may have been written in an attic or a cellar.

The Archbishop seems to hate the very idea of Progress. What has it done, he asks, to abolish drunkenness and gambling? To which we reply by asking what Christianity has done. Those vices are unmistakably here, and on the face of it any objection they may furnish against Progress must equally apply to Christianity. Nay more; for Christianity has had an unlimited opportunity to reform the world, while Progress has been hindered at every turn by the insolent usurpation of its rival.

Dr. Thomson admits that he cannot find a text in the Bible against gambling, and assuredly he cannot find one in favor of teetotalism. On the contrary he will find plenty of texts which recommend the "wine that cheereth the heart of God and man;" and he knows that his master, Jesus Christ, once played the part of an amateur publican at a marriage feast, and turned a large quantity of water into wine in order to keep the spree going when it had once begun.

We repeat that all the Archbishop's objections to Progress, based on the moral defects of men, apply with tenfold force against Religion, which has practically had the whole field to itself. And we assert that he is grievously mistaken if he imagines that supernatural beliefs can ennoble knaves or give wisdom to fools. When he talks about "Christ's blood shed to purchase our souls," and specifies the first message of his creed as "Come and be forgiven," he is appealing to our basest motives, and turning the temple into a huckster's shop. Let him and all his tribe listen to these words of Ruskin's:—

"Your honesty is not to be based either on religion or policy. Both your religion and policy must be based on it. Your honesty must be based, as the sun is, in vacant heaven; poised, as the lights in the firmament, which have rule over the day and over the night If you ask why you are to be honest—you are, in the question itself, dishonored 'Because you are a man,' is the only answer; and therefore I said in a former letter that to make your children capable of honesty is the beginning of education. Make them men first and religious men afterwards, and all will be sound; but a knave's religion is always the rottenest thing about him.—Time and Tide, p. 37."

These are the words of a real spiritual teacher. Archbishop Thomson will never get within a million miles of their meaning; nor will anybody be deceived, by the unctuous "Oh that" with which he concludes his discourse, like a mental rolling of the whites of his eyes.

As we approach the end of his address, we begin to understand his Grace's hatred of Progress. He complains that "intellectual progress never makes a man conceive eternal hopes, never makes a man conceive that he has an eternal friend in heaven, even the Son of God." Quite true. Intellectual progress tends to bound our desires within the scope of their realisation, and to dissipate the fictions of theology. It is therefore inimical to all professional soul-savers, who chatter about another world with no understanding of this; and especially to the lofty teachers of religion who luxuriate in palaces, and fling jibes and sneers at the toiling soldiers of progress who face hunger, thirst and death. These rich disciples of the poor Nazarene are horrified when the scorn is retorted on them and their creed; and Archbishop Thomson expresses his "disgust" at our ridiculing his Bible and endeavoring to bring his "convictions" into "contempt." It is, he says, "an offence against the first principles of mutual sympathy and consideration." Yet this angry complainant describes other people's convictions as "absurd and insane." All the sympathy and consideration is to be on one side! The less said about either the better. There can be no treaty or truce in a war of principles, and the soldiers of Progress will neither take quarter nor give it. Christianity must defend itself. It may try to kill us with the poisoned arrows of persecution; but what defence can it make against the rifleshot of common-sense, or how stand against the shattering artillery of science? Every such battle is decided in its commencement, for every religion begins to succumb the very moment it is attacked.

A DEFENCE OF THOMAS PAINE

(February, 1879)

Fling mud enough and some of it will stick. This noble maxim has been the favorite of traducers in all ages and climes. They know that the object of their malignity cannot always be on the alert to cleanse himself from the filth they fling, especially if cast behind his back; they know that lies, and especially slanderous lies, are hard to overtake, and when caught harder to strangle; and therefore they feel confident as to the ultimate fate of their victim if they can only persevere long enough in their vile policy of defamation. For human nature being more prone to believe evil than good of others, it generally happens that the original traducers are at length joined by a host of kindred spirits almost as eager and venomous as themselves, "the long-neck'd geese of the world, who are ever hissing dispraise because their natures are little;" while a multitude of others, not so much malignant as foolish and given to scandal, lend their cowardly assistance, and help to vilify characters far beyond the reach of their emulation. And should such characters be those of men who champion unpopular causes, there is no lie too black for belief concerning them, no accusation of secret theft or hateful meanness or loathsome lust, that will not readily gain credence. Mr. Tennyson speaks of—

> *That fierce light which beats upon a throne,*
> *And blackens every blot*

but what is that to the far fiercer and keener light which beats upon the lives of the great heroes of progress? With all due deference to the Poet Laureate, we conceive that kings and their kind have usually extended to them a charity which covers a multitude of their sins. The late king of Italy, for instance, was said to have had "the language of a guardroom, the manners of a trooper, and the morals of a he-goat," yet at his death how tenderly his faults were dealt with by the loyal press, and how strongly were all his merits brought into relief. Our own royal Sardanapalus, George the Fourth, although Leigh Hunt had the courage to describe him aright and went to the gaol for so doing, was styled by Society "the first gentleman in Europe." Yet Mazzini, Vittor Emmanuel's great contemporary, whose aims were high and noble as his life was pure, got little else than abuse from this same loyal press; and the Society which adored George the Fourth charged Shelley himself with unspeakable vices equalled only by the native turpitude of his soul.

Perhaps no man has suffered more from calumny than Thomas Paine. During his lifetime, indeed, his traducers scarcely ever dared to vent their malice in public, doubtless through fear of receiving a castigation from his vigorous and trenchant pen. But after his death they rioted in safety, and gave free play to the ingenuity of their malevolence. Gradually their libels became current; thousands of people who knew almost nothing of his life and less of his writings were persuaded that Thomas Paine, "the Infidel," was a monster of iniquity, in comparison with whom Judas appeared a saint, and the Devil himself nearly white; and this estimate finally became a tradition, which the editors of illustrated religious papers and the writers of fraudulent "Death-Bed Scenes" did their best to perpetuate. In such hands the labor of posthumous vilification might have remained without greatly troubling those who feel an interest in Thomas Paine's honor through gratitude for his work. The lowest scavengers of literature, who purvey religious offal to the dregs of orthodoxy, were better employed thus than in a reverse way, since their praise is so very much more dishonorable and appalling than their blame. But when other literary workmen of loftier repute descend to the level of these, and help them in their villainous task, it becomes advisable that some one who honors the memory of the man thus aspersed should interpose, and attempt that vindication which he can no longer make for himself.

In reviewing Mr. Edward Smith's "Life of Cobbett," our principal literary paper, the Athenæum, in its number for January 11th, went out of its way to defame Paine's character. This is what it said:—

"A more despicable man than Tom Paine cannot easily be found among the ready writers of the eighteenth century. He sold himself to the highest bidder, and he could be bought at a very low price. He wrote well; sometimes he wrote as pointedly as Junius or Cobbett. Neither excelled him in coining telling and mischievous phrases; neither surpassed him in popularity-hunting. He had the art, which was almost equal to genius, of giving happy titles to his productions. When he denounced the British Government in the name of 'Common Sense' he found willing readers in the rebellious American colonists, and a rich reward from their grateful representatives. When he wrote on behalf of the 'Rights of Man,' and in furtherance of the 'Age of Reason,' he convinced thousands by his title-pages who were incapable of perceiving the inconclusiveness of his arguments. His speculations have long since gone the way of all shams; and his charlatanism as a writer was not redeemed by his character as a man. Nothing could be worse than his private life; he was addicted to the most degrading of vices. He was no hypocrite, however, and he cannot be charged with showing that regard for appearances which constitutes the homage paid by vice to virtue. Such a man was well qualified for earning notoriety by insulting Washington. Only a thorough-paced rascal could have had the assurance to charge Washington with being unprincipled and unpatriotic. Certainly Mr. Smith has either much to learn, or else he has forgotten much, otherwise he could not venture to suggest the erection of a monument 'recording the wisdom and political virtues of Thomas Paine.'"

Now we have in this tirade all the old charges, with a new one which the critic has either furnished himself or derived from an obscure source—namely, that Paine "sold himself to the highest bidder." Let us examine the last charge first. The critic curiously contradicts himself. Paine, he admits, could "sometimes write as pointedly as Junius or Cobbett," whose works sold enormously, and he had the art of devising happy titles for his productions; yet, although he sold himself to the highest bidder, he could be bought at a very low price! The fact is, Paine was never bought at all. His was not a hireling pen. Whatever he wrote he put his name to, and he never parted with the copyright of any of his works, lest the Government or some friend of despotism should procure their suppression. He also published his writings at a ridiculously low price, so low indeed that he lost by them instead of gaining. Of his "Common Sense," that fine pamphlet which stirred the American colonists to battle against their oppressors, not less than a hundred thousand copies were sold; yet he found himself finally indebted to his printer £29 12s. 1d. Fifteen years later the English Government tried through the publisher to get the copyright of the "Rights of Man;" but though a large sum was offered, Paine refused on principle to let it pass out of his own hands. The first part of this work was published at a price which precluded any chance of profit; the publication of the second part caused him to be tried and condemned for treason, the penalty of the law being escaped only by flight. All publication of his works, whether political or religious, was afterwards illegal. Thousands of copies were circulated surreptitiously, or openly by men like Richard Carlile, who spent nine years in prison for his sale of prohibited books. But clearly Paine could derive no profit from this traffic in his works, for he never set foot in England again. Thomas Paine wrote in order to spread his political and religious views, and for no other purpose. He was not a professional author, nor a professional critic, and never needed payment for his literary work. And assuredly he got none. Let the Athenæum critic inform the world to whom Paine sold himself, or who ever paid him a penny for his writings. Until he does so we shall believe that the author of "Common Sense," the "Rights of Man," and the "Age of Reason," was honest in saying: "In a great affair, where the good of mankind is at stake, I love to work for nothing; and so fully am I under the influence of this principle, that I should lose the spirit, the pride, and the pleasure of it, were I conscious that I looked for reward."

Popularity-hunting, to use the critic's graceless phrase, was Paine's next fault; but as, according to the same authority, he was guilty in this respect only in the same sense as Junius was, the burden of his iniquity cannot be very great.

Addiction to the most degrading of vices, is a charge difficult to confute until we know specifically what vice is meant. Paine has been accused of drunkenness; but by whom? Not by his intimate acquaintances, who would have detected his guilt, but by his enemies who were never in his society, and therefore could know nothing of his habits. Cheetham, who first disseminated this accusation, was a notorious libeller, and was more than once compelled to make a public apology for his lies; but he was a shameless creature, and actually in his "Life" of Paine resuscitated and amplified falsehoods for which he had tendered abject apologies while his victim was alive. Even, however, if Paine had yielded to the seductions of strong drink, he should be judged by the custom of his own age, and not that of ours.

Mr. Leslie Stephen does not rail against Boswell for his drinking powers; Burns is not outlawed for his devotion to John Barlycorn; Byron and Sheridan are not beyond pardon because they often went drunk to bed; and some of the greatest statesmen of last century and this, including Pitt and Fox, are not considered the basest of men because they exercised that right which Major O'Gorman claims for all Irishmen—"to drink as much as they can carry." But no such plea is necessary, for Paine was not addicted to drink, but remarkably abstemious. Mr. Fellows, with whom he lived for more than six months, said that he never saw him the worse for drink. Dr. Manley said, "while I attended him he never was inebriated." Colonel Burr said, "he was decidedly temperate." And even Mr. Jarvis, whom Cheetham cited as his authority for charging Paine with drunkenness, authorised Mr. Vale, of New York, editor of the Beacon, to say that Cheetham lied. Amongst the public men who knew Paine personally were Burke, Home Tooke, Priestley, Lord Edward Fitzgerald, Dr. Moore, Jefferson, Washington, Volney and Condorcet: but none of these ever hinted at his love of drink. The charge of drunkeness is a posthumous libel, circulated by a man who had publicly quarrelled with Paine, who had been obliged to apologise for former aspersions, and who after Paine's death was prosecuted and condemned for libelling a lady whom he had accused of undue familiarity with the principal object of his malice.

Finding the charge of drunkenness unequivocally rebutted, Paine's traducers advance that of licentiousness. But this is equally unsuccessful. The authority relied on is still Cheetham, who in turn borrowed from a no less disreputable source. A man named Carver had quarrelled with Paine over money matters; in fact, he had been obliged with a loan which he forgot to pay, and like all base natures he showed his gratitude to his benefactor, when no more favors could be expected, by hating and maligning him. A scurrilous letter written by this fellow fell into the hands of Cheetham, who elaborated it in his "Life." It broadly hinted that Madame Bonneville, the by no means youthful wife of a Paris bookseller who had sheltered Paine when he was threatened with danger in that city, was his paramour; for no other reason than that he had in turn sheltered her when she repaired with her children to America, after her home had been broken up by Buonaparte's persecution of her husband. This lady prosecuted Cheetham for libel, and a jury of American citizens gave her a verdict and damages.

Here the matter might rest, but we are inclined to urge another consideration. No one of his many enemies ever accused Paine of licentiousness in his virile manhood; and can we believe that he began a career of licentiousness in his old age, when, besides the infirmities natural to his time of life, he suffered dreadful tortures from an internal abscess brought on by his confinement in the reeking dungeons of the Luxembourg, which made life a terror and death a boon? Only lunatics or worse would credit such a preposterous story.

The Athenoum critic alleges that Paine insulted Washington, and was therefore a "thorough-paced rascal." But he did nothing of the kind. He very properly remonstrated with Washington for coolly allowing him to rot in a French dungeon for no crime except that he was a foreigner, when a word from the President of the United States, of which he was a citizen, would have effected his release.

Washington was aware of Paine's miserable plight, yet he forgot the obligations of friendship; and notwithstanding frequent letters from Munro, the American ambassador at Paris, he supinely suffered the man he had once delighted to honor to languish in wretchedness, filth, and disease. George Washington did much for American Independence, but Thomas Paine did perhaps more, for his writings animated the oppressed Colonists with an enthusiasm for liberty without which the respectable generalship of Washington might have been exerted in vain. The first President of the United States was, as Carlyle grimly says, "no immeasurable man," and we conceive that Paine had earned the right to criticise even him and his policy.

Every person is of course free to hold what opinion he pleases of Paine's writings. The Athenoum critic thinks they have "gone the way of all shams." He is wrong in fact, for they circulate very extensively still. And he may also be wrong in his literary judgment. William Hazlitt, whose opinion on any subject connected with literature is at least as valuable as an Athenoum critic's, ranked Paine very high as a political writer, and affirmed of his "Rights of Man" that it was "a powerful and explicit reply to Burke." But Hazlitt had read Paine, which we suspect many glib critics of to-day have not; for we well remember how puzzled some of them were to explain whence Shelley took the motto "We pity the Plumage, but Forget the Dying Bird" prefixed to his Address to the People on the death of the Princess Charlotte. It was taken, as they should have known, from one of the finest passages of the "Rights of Man." Critics, it is well known, sometimes write as Artemus Ward proposed to lecture on science, "with an imagination untrammeled by the least knowledge of the subject."

Let us close this vindication of Paine by citing the estimate of him formed by Walt Whitman, an authority not to be sneered at now even by Athenoum critics. In 1877 the Liberal League of Philadelphia celebrated the 140th birthday of Thomas Paine, and a large audience was gathered by the announcement that Whitman would speak. The great poet, according to the Index report, after telling how he had become intimate with some of Paine's friends thirty-five years before, went on to say:—

"I dare not say how much of what our Union is owning and enjoying to-day, its independence, its ardent belief in, and substantial practice of, Radical human rights, and the severance of its Government from all ecclesiastical and superstitious dominion— I dare not say how much of all this is owing to Thomas Paine; but I am inclined to think a good portion of it decidedly is. Of the foul and foolish fictions yet told about the circumstances of his decease, the absolute fact is that, as he lived a good life after its kind, he died calmly, philosophically, as became him. He served the embryo Union with the most precious service, a service that every man, woman, and child in the thirty-eight States is to some extent receiving the benefit of to-day, and I for one here cheerfully and reverently throw one pebble on the cairn of his memory."

We are content to let the reader decide between Whitman and the Athenoum critic in their respective estimates of him who wrote, and as we think acted up to it—"All the world is my country, and to do good my religion."

THE GOSPEL OF FREETHOUGHT

(August, 1882)

Christians are perpetually crying that we destroy and never build up. Nothing could be more false, for all negation has a positive side, and we cannot deny error without affirming truth. But even if it were true, it would not lessen the value of our work. You must clear the ground before you can build, and plough before you sow. Splendor gives no strength to an edifice whose foundations are treacherous, nor can a harvest be reaped from fields unprepared for the seed.

Freethought is, in this respect, like a skilful physician, whose function it is to expel disease and leave the patient sound and well. No sick man claims that the doctor shall supply him with something in place of his malady. It is enough that the enemy of his health is driven out. He is then in a position to act for himself. He has legs to walk with, a brain to devise, and hands to execute his will. What more does he need? What more can he ask without declaring himself a weakling or a fool? So it is with superstition, the deadliest disease of the mind. Free-thought casts it out, with its blindness and its terrors, and leaves the mind clear and free. All nature is then before us to study and enjoy. Truth shines on us with celestial light, Goodness smiles on our best endeavors, and Beauty thrills our senses and kindles our imagination with the subtle magic of her charms.

What a boon it is to think freely, to let the intellect dart out in quest of truth at every point of the compass, to feel the delight of the chase and the gladness of capture! What a noble privilege to pour treasures of knowledge into the crucible of the brain, and separate gold from the dross!

The Freethinker takes nothing on trust, if he can help it; he dissects, analyses, and proves everything. Does this make him a barren sceptic? Not so. What he discards he knows to be worthless, and he also knows the value of what he prizes. If one sweet vision turns out a mirage, how does it lessen our enjoyment at the true oasis, or shake our certitude of water and shade under the palm trees by the well?

The masses of men do not think freely. They scarcely think at all out of their round of business. They are trained not to think. From the cradle to the grave orthodoxy has them in its clutches. Their religion is settled by priests, and their political and social institutions by custom. They look askance at the man who dares to question what is established; not reflecting that all orthodoxies were once heterodox, that without innovation there could never have been any progress, and that if inquisitive fellows had not gone prying about in forbidden quarters ages ago, the world would still be peopled by savages dressed in nakedness, war-paint, and feathers. The mental stultification which begins in youth reaches ossification as men grow older. Lack of thought ends in incapacity to think.

Real Freethought is impossible without education. The mind cannot operate without means or construct without materials. Theology opposes education: Freethought supports it. The poor as well as the rich should share in its blessings. Education is a social capital which should be supplied to all. It enriches and expands. It not only furnishes the mind, but strengthens its faculties. Knowledge is power. A race of giants could not level the Alps; but ordinary men, equipped with science, bore through their base, and made easy channels for the intercourse of divided nations.

Growth comes with use, and power with exercise. Education makes both possible. It puts the means of salvation at the service of all, and, prevents the faculties from moving about in vacuo, and finally standing still from sheer hopelessness. The educated man has a whole magazine of appliances at his command, and his intellect is trained in using them, while the uneducated man has nothing but his strength, and his training is limited to its use.

Freethought demands education for all. It claims a mental inheritance for every child born into the world. Superstition demands ignorance, stupidity, and degradation. Wherever the schoolmaster is busy, Freethought prospers; where he is not found, superstition reigns supreme and levels the people in the dust.

Free speech and Freethought go together. If one is hampered the other languishes. What is the use of thinking if I may not express my thought? We claim equal liberty for all. The priest shall say what he believes and so shall the sceptic. No law shall protect the one and disfranchise the other. If any man disapproves what I say, he need not hear me a second time. What more does he require? Let him listen to what he likes, and leave others to do the same. Let us have justice and fair play all round.

Freethought is not only useful but laudable. It involves labor and trouble. Ours is not a gospel for those who love the soft pillow of faith. The Freethinker does not let his ship rot away in harbor; he spreads his canvas and sails the seas of thought. What though tempests beat and billows roar? He is undaunted, and leaves the avoidance of danger to the sluggard and the slave. He will not pay their price for ease and safety. Away he sails with Vigilance at the prow and Wisdom at the helm. He not only traverses the ocean highways, but skirts unmapped coasts and ventures on uncharted seas. He gathers spoils in every zone, and returns with a rich freight that compensates for all hazards. Some day or other, you say, he will be shipwrecked and lost. Perhaps. All things end somehow. But if he goes down he will die like a man and not like a coward, and have for his requiem the psalm of the tempest and the anthem of the waves.

Doubt is the beginning of wisdom. It means caution, independence, honesty and veracity. Faith means negligence, serfdom, insincerity and deception. The man who never doubts never thinks. He is like a straw in the wind or a waif on the sea. He is one of the helpless, docile, unquestioning millions, who keep the world in a state of stagnation, and serve as a fulcrum for the lever of despotism. The stupidity of the people, says Whitman, is always inviting the insolence of power.

Buckle has well said that scepticism is "the necessary antecedent of all progress." Without it we should still be groping in the night of the Dark Ages. The very foundations of modern science and philosophy were laid on ground which was wrested from the Church, and every stone was cemented with the blood of martyrs. As the edifice arose the sharpshooters of faith attacked the builders at every point, and they still continue their old practice, although their missiles can hardly reach the towering heights where their enemies are now at work.

Astronomy was opposed by the Church because it unsettled old notions of the earth being the centre of the universe, and the sun, moon, and stars mere lights stuck in the solid firmament, and worked to and fro like sliding panels. Did not the Bible say that General Joshua commanded the sun to stand still, and how could this have happened unless it moved round the earth? And was not the earth certainly flat, as millions of flats believed it to be? The Catholic Inquisition forced Galileo to recant, and Protestant Luther called Copernicus "an old fool."

Chemistry was opposed as an impious prying into the secrets of God. It was put in the same class with sorcery and witchcraft, and punished in the same way. The early chemists were considered as agents of the Devil, and their successors are still regarded as "uncanny" in the more ignorant parts of Christendom. Roger Bacon was persecuted by his brother monks; his testing fire was thought to have come from the pit, and the explosion of his gunpowder was the Devil vanishing in smoke and smell. Even at the end of last century, the clergy-led mob of Birmingham who wrecked Priestley's house and destroyed his apparatus, no doubt felt that there was a close connexion between chemistry and infidelity.

Physiology and Medicine were opposed on similar grounds. We were all fearfully and wonderfully made, and the less the mystery was looked into the better. Disease was sent by God for his own wise ends, and to resist it was as bad as blasphemy. Every discovery and every reform was decried as impious. Men now living can remember how the champions of faith denounced the use of anaesthetics in painful labor as an interference with God's curse on the daughters of Eve.

Geology was opposed because it discredited Moses, as though that famous old Jew had watched the deposit of every stratum of the earth's crust. It was even said that fossils had been put underground by God to puzzle the wiseacres, and that the Devil had carried shells to the hilltops for the purpose of deluding men to infidelity and perdition. Geologists were anathematised from the pulpits and railed at by tub-thumpers. They were obliged to feel their way and go slowly. Sir Charles Lyell had to keep back his strongest conclusions for at least a quarter of a century, and could not say all he thought until his head was whitened by old age and he looked into the face of Death.

Biology was opposed tooth and nail as the worst of all infidelity. It exposed Genesis and put Moses out of court. It destroyed all special creation, showed man's kinship with other forms of life, reduced Adam and Eve to myths, and exploded the doctrine of the Fall. Darwin was for years treated as Antichrist, and Huxley as the great beast. All that is being changed, thanks to the sceptical spirit. Darwin's corpse is buried in Westminster Abbey, but his ideas are undermining all the churches and crumbling them into dust.

The gospel of Freethought brands persecution as the worst crime against humanity. It stifles the spirit of progress and strangles its pioneers. It eliminates the brave, the adventurous and the aspiring, and leaves only the timid, the sluggish and the grovelling. It removes the lofty and spares the low. It levels all the hills of thought and makes an intellectual flatness. It drenches all the paths of freedom with blood and tears, and makes earth the vestibule of hell.

Persecution is the right arm of priestcraft. The black militia of theology are the sworn foes of Freethought. They represent it as the sin against the Holy Ghost, for which there is no forgiveness in this world or the next. When they speak of the Holy Ghost they mean themselves. Freethought is a crime against them. It strips off the mystery that invests their craft, and shows them as they really are, a horde of bandits who levy black mail on honest industry, and preach a despot in heaven in order to main-tain their own tyranny on earth.

The gospel of Freethought would destroy all priesthoods. Every man should be his own priest. If a professional soul-doctor gives you wrong advice and leads you to ruin, he will not be damned for you He will see you so first. We must take all responsibility, and we should also take the power. Instead of putting our thinking out, as we put our washing, let us do it at home. No man can do another's thinking for him. What is thought in the originator is only acquiescence in the man who takes it at secondhand.

If we do our own thinking in religion we shall do it in everything else. We reject authority and act for ourselves. Spiritual and temporal power are brought under the same rule. They must justify themselves or go. The Freethinker is thus a politician and a social reformer. What a Christian may be he must be. Freethinkers are naturally Radicals. They are almost to a man on the side of justice freedom and progress. The Tories know this, and hence they seek to suppress us by the violence of unjust law. They see that we are a growing danger to every kind of privilege, a menace to all the idle classes who live in luxury on the sweat and labor of others—the devouring drones who live on the working bees.

The gospel of Freethought teaches us to distinguish between the knowable and the unknowable. We cannot fathom the infinite "mystery of the universe" with our finite plummet, nor see aught behind the veil of death. Here is our appointed province:

> *"This world which is the world*
> *Of all of us, and where in the end*
> *We find our happiness or not at all."*

Let us make the best of this world and take our chance of any other. If there is a heaven, we dare say it will hold all honest men. If it will not, those who go elsewhere will at least be in good company.

Our salvation is here and now. It is certain and not contingent. We need not die before we realise it. Ours is a gospel, and the only gospel, for this side of the grave. The promises of theology cannot be made good till after death; ours are all redeemable in this life.

We ask men to acknowledge realities and dismiss fictions. When you have sifted all the learned sermons ever preached, you will find very little good grain. Theology deals with dreams and phantasies, and gives no guidance to practical men. The whole truth of life may be summed up in a few words. Happiness is the only good, suffering the only evil, and selfishness the only sin. And the whole duty of man may be expressed in one sentence, slightly altered from Voltaire—Learn what is true in order to do what is right. If a man can tell you anything about these matters, listen to him; if not, turn a deaf ear, and let him preach to the wind.

The only noble things in this world are great hearts and great brains, There is no virtue in a starveling piety which turns all beauty into ugliness and shrivels up every natural affection. Let the heart beat high with courage and enterprise, and throb with warm passion. Let the brain be an active engine of thought, imagination and will. The gospel of sorrow has had its day, and the time has come for the gospel of gladness. Let us live out our lives to the full, radiating joy on all in our own circle, and diffusing happiness through the grander circle of humanity, until at last we retire from the banquet of life, as others have done before us, and sink in eternal repose.

FREETHOUGHT IN CURRENT LITERATURE

[A Paper read at the Annual Conference of the National Secular Society, in the Co-operative Hall, Bury, June 5th, 1881.]

When I was invited to read a paper at this Conference, I thought that, as editor of the Freethinker, I ought to say something about Freethonght. And as the deliberations of this Conference are mostly on practical matters, it occurred to me that I had better select a subject of less immediate though not of insignificant interest. So I resolved to address you on Freethonght in Current Literature.

I have said that this subject, if not practical and urgent, is assuredly not unimportant. The power of literature over men's minds cannot be estimated too highly. Science is a tremendous force, but its greatest influence is exercised over the human mind when it quits the merely practical task of ministering to our material desires, and seeks to mould our moral and spiritual conceptions of our position and destiny in the universe. To do this it must address us through the medium of literature. Art also is a great force, more especially in countries which have not been subjected, like ours, to the bondage of Puritanism. But art has hitherto appealed to a restricted circle, although that circle is rapidly widening in our own age. The greatest, most permanent, and most universal force is literature. Raphael and Michael Angelo have not influenced the world so profoundly as Shakespeare and Dante; while so many artistic achievements of antiquity are lost or half decayed, its literary masterpieces still survive with undiminished freshness and charm;

and while the most eminent works even of contemporary artists are seen only occasionally by a few, the most eminent writings of the world's master minds may and do become a household possession to thousands who move in the humblest spheres of life.

In these cosmopolitan days the Freethinker and Humanitarian naturally looks beyond his own country into the great world, which is at present divided by national and other barriers, but which will in time become the home of one all-embracing family. And I confess that I was strongly tempted to trace the workings of the spirit of Freethought as far as I could in the general literature of Europe. But I soon recognised the necessity of limiting myself to the manifestations of that subtle and pervasive spirit in the current literature of our English tongue.

When the present century commenced Europe was stirred to the utter depths by that great French Revolution which marked a new epoch in the world's history. The revolutionary wave surged across the western world, and passed over England as well as other countries. Some thought the huge eclipse of social order which accompanied it the herald of approaching night, and others thought it the dawn of a new day; but none were indifferent. There was an intense excitement of radical passions and desires, a quickening of all the springs of life. This produced a blossoming of our literature such as had not been witnessed since the great Elizabethan age, and then, as before, Free-thought mixed with the vital sap. Of the long array of post-revolutionary names I select three—Thomas Paine, who represented the keen and restless common-sense of Freethought; William Godwin, who represented its calmer philosophy; and Shelley, who represented its lofty hopes and soaring aspirations. Godwin has almost faded into a name; Paine's great work is nearly done, for a deeper and more scientific scepticism has possessed itself of the field in which he labored; but Shelley has a message for generations yet unborn. He emerges as the supreme figure destined to immortality of fame. All great and noble and beautiful qualities cohere in him, the "poet of poets and purest of men." And he is ours. Byron, with all his splendid energy and terrible scorn, quailed before the supreme problems of life; but Shelley faced them with a courage all the greater because it was unconscious, and casting aside all superstitious dreams and illusory hopes, yearned prophetically towards the Future, when freedom, truth and love shall supersede all other trinities, and realise here on earth that Paradise which theologians have only promised in a world to come.

A Shelley cultus has grown up during recent years, and many of our most gifted writers reverently bow themselves before him. I have only to mention such names as Browning, Swinburne, and Rossetti to show the intellectual rank of his worshippers. Their number increases every year, and it is touching to witness the avidity with which they seize on all new facts relating to him, whether the record of some episode in his life, a reported conversation, or a scrap of writing from his hand.

From the Shelley and Byron period to the fresh revolutionary outburst of 1848 there was a lull in England as well as elsewhere. Several great political reforms were achieved in the interval. A Reform Bill was carried. Catholics and Jews were emancipated, and freedom and cheapness of the press were won by the untameable courage of men like Carlile, Hetherington, Lovett, and Watson. But quietude reigned in the higher spheres of literature. The age was eminently respectable, and it acclaimed the highly respectable Wordsworth as, the prophet divinely inspired to teach men how to rest and be thankful.

But during that interval of apathy and respectability, Science was slowly gathering strength and making conquests, in preparation for the time when she might plant her feet firmly on the solid ground she had won, and challenge Theology to mortal combat. Geology and Biology, in especial, were getting themselves ready to overthrow the fables of Genesis and destroy its doctrines of special creation. And one is glad to admit that they have completely succeeded at last. Professor Huxley declares that he is not acquainted with any man of science or properly instructed person who believes that Adam and Eve were the first parents of mankind, or that we have all descended from the eight persons who superintended that wonderful floating menagerie which survived a universal deluge less than five thousand years ago. And all the clergy can say in reply is that Professor Huxley is not endowed with that theological faculty which enables them to perceive in the language of Scripture a meaning which is quite undiscernible to the eyes of common sense.

Another influence was at work during that interval. Mainly through Carlyle, the treasures of German literature were opened up to English readers. The greatest German writers, from Leasing, Göethe, and Schiller to Fichte, Richter, and Heine, were outrageous Freethinkers compared with our own respectable and orthodox writers, and their influence soon made itself evident in the tolerance and courage with which English authors began to treat the great problems of morality and religion. German scholarship, too, slowly crept among us. Its Biblical criticism showed us the utter inadequacy of evidential works like Paley's, and made us see that the Christian Scriptures would have to be viewed in a very different light and studied in a very different spirit. To estimate the extent of this change, we have only to place Paley's "Evidences of

Christianity" beside such a work as "Supernatural Religion." The gulf between these works is enormous; and it is notable that the more scientific and rigorous is the criticism of the New Testament books, the more heterodox are the conclusions reached. Even Scotland has been invaded by this German influence, and it now affords us the laughable spectacle of a number of grave ministers pursuing as a damnable heretic a man like Dr. Robertson Smith, whose only crime is having stated about the Bible nothing new, but what every scholar in Europe knows to be admitted and indisputable. These solemn ministers of the old creed are determined to keep the deluge of what they call "German infidelity" from flooding the valleys and mounting the hillsides of Scotland; but their heresy-hunts are just as efficacious against what they so piously dread as Mrs. Partington's mop against the mighty onrush of Atlantic rollers.

With the revolutionary movement of '48 came a fresh impulse from France. The great evangel of '89 had not perished; it was only in abeyance; and again it burst upon Europe with its words of fire. We all know how the Republic which was then established was soon suppressed in blood by the gang of adventurers presided over by Napoleon the Little. But the day of retribution came, and the empire went the way of all tyrannies. On its ruins the Republic has been established anew, and now it reckons in its service and among its champions the best intellects and the noblest characters in France; while the masses of the people, taught by the bitter lessons of adversity, are also content to enjoy the benefits of ordered liberty and peaceful progress under its benign sway.

Now French progress has always been a question of ideas no less than of material advantage. The great democratic leaders in France have nearly all been avowed Freethinkers. They have separated themselves alike from "the blood on the hands of the king and the lie at the lips of the priest," being perfectly assured that outward freedom in politics is in the long run impossible without inward freedom of thought. The chief statesman in France, M. Gambetta, has publicly declared himself a disciple of Voltaire, and neither at the marriages nor at the funerals of his friends does he ever enter the doors of a church. He stays outside and quietly allows those who desire it to go in and listen to the mumbling of the priest.

My purpose, however, being literary and not political, I must recur to my remark that a fresh impulse came to us from France after the revolution of '48. Lamartine at first exercised considerable influence here, but gradually Victor Hugo's star ascended, and from the moment it reached the zenith until now, he has been accounted the supreme poet of France, and the greatest contemporary evangelist of the ideas of '89. He is a Freethinker as well as a Republican; and it was inevitable that the younger school of writers in England, who acknowledge him as a lofty master, should drink from his inexhaustible spring the living waters of Democracy and Freethought.

French influence on our very recent literature is evident in such works as Mr. John Morley's Studies on Voltaire, Rousseau, Diderot, and Condorcet; Mr. Christie's monumental Life of Etienne Dolet, the Freethought martyr; and Mr. Parton's new Life of Voltaire; all of which demand and will amply requite our attention.

Such are the influences which have conspired to shape the literary activities of the generation in which we live. Now Freethought, like a subtle essence, penetrates everywhere. Every book betrays its presence, and even the periodical literature of our age is affected by it. The Archbishop of Canterbury laments that Christian men cannot introduce the most respectable magazines into their homes without the risk of poisoning the minds of their families with heretical ideas.

One of the signs that Freethought had begun to leaven the educated classes was the publication of the famous "Essays and Reviews." The heresy of that book was exceedingly small, but it roused a great storm in the religious world and led to more than one clerical prosecution. Another sign was the publication of Colenso's learned work on the Pentateuch. This hard-working Colonial Bishop was denounced as a heretic by the idler home Bishops, and Ruskin has said that they would have liked to burn Colenso alive, and make Ludgate Hill easier for the omnibuses with the cinders of him. An antagonist very different from the Bishops was Mr. Matthew Arnold, who severely censured Colenso's whole method of criticism, as a handling of religious questions in an irreligious spirit. Mr. W. R. Greg admirably defended the Bishop, and the controversy ended in a drawn battle.

But what has happened since? The same Matthew Arnold who censured Colenso has himself published two remarkable works on "Literature and Dogma" and "God and the Bible," written it is true on a different plan from Colenso's, but containing a hundred times more heresy than the Bishop crammed into all his big volumes. For Mr. Arnold deprecates the idea of a personal god, likens the Christian Trinity to three Lord Shaftesburys, and says that the Bible miracles must all be given up without reservation. All the positive religion he leaves us is the belief in "An eternal not ourselves that makes for righteousness," which is about as nebulous a creed as ever was preached. Now Mr. Arnold is not an insignificant person. He is recognised as a past-master of English letters, a ripe scholar, a fine poet, and an exquisite critic. When such a man carries destructive criticism to its utmost limits, we may well congratulate ourselves on a signal triumph of Freethought. And we may also find comfort in the fact that nobody thinks of flinging a stone at Mr. Arnold for his heresy. By-and-by the censors of religion in the press will cease to throw stones at the Freethought teachers among the masses of the people, who only put into homlier English and publish in a cheaper form the sentiments and ideas which Mr. Arnold expresses for the educated classes at a higher price and in a loftier style.

During the winter a gap was made in the front rank of English literature by the deaths of Carlyle and George Eliot. Neither of these great writers was orthodox. Carlyle was a Freethinker to the extent of discarding Christian supernaturalism. Very early in his life he told Edward Irving that he did not, nor was it likely he ever would, regard Christianity as he did. We all remember, too, his scornful references to Hebrew Old Clothes, and his fierce diatribes against the clergy who, he said, went about with strange gear on their heads, and underneath it such a theory of the universe as he, for one, was thankful to have no concern with. In the "Latter-Day Pamphlets" he likened Christianity to a great tree, sprung from the seed of Nazareth, and since fed by the opulences of fifty generations; which now is perishing at the root, and sways to and fro ever farther and farther from the perpendicular; and which in the end must come down, and leave to those who found shelter beneath it and thought it infinite, a wholesome view of the upper eternal lights. And his contempt for controversial or dogmatic theology may be gauged by his reply to one who asked him whether he was a Pantheist. "No," said Carlyle, "never was; nor a Pot-Theist either."

George Eliot was notoriously a Freethinker. Early in her literary career she translated Strauss and Feuerback into English, and through all her novels there runs a profound Secular spirit. Among her friends she was well known to be a Positivist; and though her creed held forth no promise of personal life beyond the grave, she found inspiration and comfort in the thought that Humanity would advance after she was gone, that though she died the race was practically immortal. Her mind was thoroughly imbued with the scientific spirit, and her writings give some conception of the way in which the Evolution theory affected a mind, fortified by culture and abundant common sense against the crudities of enthusiasm. The doctrine of Evolution did not fill her with despair; on the contrary, it justified and strengthened her ardent hopes for the future of mankind.

Many other novelists betray a strong spirit of Freethought.

It pervades all George Meredith's later writings, and is still more conspicuous in Mrs. Lynn Linton's "True History of Joshua Davidson" and her powerful "Under which Lord?" the hero-husband of that story being an Agnostic gentleman who founds a workmen's institute and delivers Freethought lectures in it.

Almost all the young school of poets are Freethinkers. Browning, our greatest, and Tennyson, our most popular, belong to a generation that is past. Mr. Swinburne is at the head of the new school, and he is a notorious heretic. He never sings more loftily, or with stronger passion, or with finer thought, than when he arraigns and denounces priestcraft and its superstitions before the bar of humanity and truth.

The reception of Mr. Thomsons poems and essays affords another sign of the progress of Freethought. This gentleman for many years contributed to secular journals under the initials of "B. V." He is a pronounced Atheist, and makes no concealment of it in his poems.

Yet, while a few critics have expressed horror at his heresy, the majority have treated it as extremely natural in an educated thoughtful man, and confined themselves to the task of estimating the genius he has put into his work.

I must now draw to a close. Freethought, I hold, is an omnipresent active force in the English literature of to-day. It appears alike in the greatest works of scholarship, in the writings of men of science, in the songs of poets, in the productions of novelists, in the most respectable magazines, and in the multitudinous daily press. It is urgent and aggressive, and tolerates no restraint. It indicates the progress we have made towards that time when the mind of man shall play freely on every subject, when no question shall be thought too sacred to be investigated, when reason shall be the sovereign arbiter of all disputes, when priestly authority shall have perished, when every man's thought shall decide his own belief, and his conscience determine the way in which he shall walk.

DEAN STANLEY'S LATEST

(August, 1880)

At one of Charles Lamb's delightful Wednesday evenings Coleridge had, as usual, consumed more than his fair share of time in talking of some "regenerated" orthodoxy. Leigh Hunt, who was one of the listeners, manifested his surprise at the prodigality and intensity of the poet's religious expressions, and especially at his always speaking of Jesus as "our Savior." Whereupon Lamb, slightly exhilarated by a glass of gooseberry cordial, stammered out, "Ne—ne—never mind what Coleridge says; he's full of fun." This jocular and irreverent criticism is perhaps, after all, the most pertinent that can be passed on the utterances of this school of "regenerated orthodoxy." Coleridge, who had unbounded genius, and was intellectually capable of transforming British philosophy, went on year after year maundering about his "sumject" and "omject," mysteriously alluding to his great projected work on the Logos, and assuring everybody that he knew a way of bringing all ascertained truth within the dogmas of the Church of England. His pupil, Maurice, wasted a noble intellect (as Mill says, few of his contemporaries had so much intellect to waste) in the endeavor to demonstrate that the Thirty-Nine Articles really anticipated all the extremest conclusions of modern thought; afflicting himself perpetually, as has been well said, with those "forty stripes save one." And now we have Dean Stanley, certainly a much smaller man than Maurice, and infinitely smaller than Coleridge, continuing the traditions of the school, of which let us hope he will be the last teacher. What his theology precisely is no mortal can determine. He subscribes the doctrines of the Church of England, but then he interprets them in an esoteric sense; that is, of course, in a Stanleyan sense; for when the letter of doctrine is left for its occult meaning every man "runs" a private interpretation of his own. The Nineteenth Century for August contains a characteristic specimen of his exegesis. It is entitled "The Creed of the Early Christians," but is really a sermon on the Trinity, which doubtless has been preached at Westminster. We shall examine its peculiarities and try to reach its meaning; a task by no means easy, and one which we could pardon anyone for putting aside with Lamb's remark, "It's only his fun."

Dean Stanley has a new theory of the Trinity, partly deduced from other mystics, and partly constructed on the plan of the negro who explained that his wooden doll was made "all by myself, out of my own head." God the Father, in this as in other theories, comes first: not that he is older or greater than the other persons, for they are all three coequal and coëternal; but because you must have a first for the sake of enumeration, or else the most blessed Trinity would be like the Irishman's little pig who ran about so that there was no counting him. There is also another reason. God the Father corresponds to Natural Religion, which of course has priority in the religious development of mankind; coming before Revealed Religion, to which God the Son corresponds, and still more before Spiritual Religion to which corresponds the Holy Ghost.

"We look round the physical world; we see indications of order, design, and good will towards the living creatures which animate it. Often, it is true, we cannot trace any such design; but, whenever we can, the impression upon us is the sense of a Single, Wise, Beneficent Mind, the same now that it was ages before the appearance of man—the same in other parts of the Universe as it is in our own. And in our own hearts and consciences we feel an instinct corresponding to this—a voice, a faculty, that seems to refer us to a higher power than ourselves, and to point to some Invisible Sovereign Will, like to that which we see impressed on the natural world. And further, the more we think of the Supreme, the more we try to imagine what his feelings are towards us, the more our idea of him becomes fixed as in the one simple, all-embracing word that he is Our Father."

The words we have italicised say that design cannot always be traced in nature. We should like to know where it can ever be. Evolution shows that the design argument puts the cart before the horse. Natural Selection, as Dr. Schmidt appositely remarks, accounts for adaptation as a result without requiring the supposition of design as a cause. And if you cannot deduce God from the animate world, you are not likely to deduce him from the inanimate. Dean Stanley himself quotes some remarkable words from Dr. Newman's Apologia—"The being of a god is as certain to me as the certainty of my own existence. Yet when I look out of myself into the world of men, I see a sight which fills me with unspeakable distress. The world of men seems simply to give the lie to that great truth of which my whole being is so full. If I looked into a mirror and did not see my face, I should experience the same sort of difficulty that actually comes upon me when I look into this living busy world and see no reflection of its Creator." How, asks the Dean, is this difficulty to be met? Oh, he replies, I we must turn to God the Son in the person of Jesus Christ, and his utterances will supplement and correct the uncertain sounds of nature; and then there is the Holy Ghost to finally supply all omissions, and clear up all difficulties. Now to our mind this is simply intellectual thimble-rigging. Or rather does it not suggest the three-card trick? One card is useless, two cards are unsafe, but with three cards to shuffle you are almost sure to win. Dr. Newman gets his God through intuition; he maintains that the existence of God is a primary fact of consciousness, and entirely declines the impossible task of proving it from the phænomena of nature. Dean Stanley should do the same. It is not honest to employ an argument and then shirk all the difficulties it raises by resorting to the theological three-card trick, which confounds instead of satisfying the spectator, while emptying his mental pockets of the good cash of common sense.

The Dean's treatment of God the Son is amusing. He writes of Jesus Christ as though he were a principle instead of a person. "The Mahometan," he says, "rightly objects to the introduction of the paternal and filial relations into the idea of God, when they are interpreted in the gross and literal sense. But in the moral spiritual sense it is true that the kindness, tenderness and wisdom we find in Jesus Christ is the reflection of the same kindness, tenderness and wisdom which we recognise in the governance of the universe." This may be called mysticism, but we think it moonshine. Gross and literal sense, forsooth! Why, was not Jesus Christ a man, a most literal fact, "gross as a mountain, open, palpable?" Dean Stanley approves the Mahometan's objection, and yet he knows full well that it contravenes a fundamental dogma of the Christian Church, and is accounted a most damnable heresy. Why this paltering with us in a double sense? To our mind downright blatant orthodoxy, which is at least honest if not subtle, is preferable to this hybrid theology which attempts to reconcile contradictions in order to show respect to truth while sticking to the flesh-pots of error, and evades all difficulties by a patent and patently dishonest method of "interpretation."

Quoting Goethe's "Wilhelm Meister," Dean Stanley tells us that one great benefit traceable to God the Son is the recognition of "humility and poverty, mockery and despising, wretchedness and suffering, as divine." Well, if these things are divine, the sooner we all become devilish the better. Nobody thinks them divine when they happen to himself; on the contrary, he cries out lustily against them. But it is a different matter when they happen to others. Then the good Christian considers them divine. How easily, says a French wit, we bear other people's troubles! Undistracted by personal care, pious souls contemplate with serene resignation the suffering of their neighbors, and acknowledge in them the chastening hand of a Divine Father.

God the Holy Ghost represents Spiritual religion: the Father represents God in Nature, the Son represents God in History, and "the Holy Ghost represents to us God in our own hearts and spirits and consciences." Here be truths! An illustration is given. Theodore Parker, when a boy, took up a stone to throw at a tortoise in a pond, but felt himself restrained by something within him; and that something, as his mother told him, was the voice of God, or in other words the Holy Ghost. Now if the Holy Ghost is required to account for every kind impulse of boys and men, there is required also an Unholy Ghost to account for all our unkind impulses. That is, a place in theology must be found for the Devil. The equilateral triangle of theology must be turned into a square, with Old Nick for the fourth side. But Dean Stanley does not like the Devil; he deems him not quite respectable enough for polite society. Let him, then, give up the Holy Ghost too, for the one is the correlative of the other.

"It may be," says the Dean, after interpreting the Trinity, "that the Biblical words in some respects fall short of this high signification." What, God's own language inferior to that of the Dean of Westminster? Surely this is strange arrogance, unless after all "it's only his fun." Perhaps that is how we should take it. Referring to some sacred pictures in the old churches of the East on Mount Athos, intended to represent the doctrine of the Trinity, the Dean says that standing on one side the spectator sees only Christ on the Cross, standing on the other he sees only the Holy Dove, while standing in front he sees only the Eternal Father. Very admirable, no doubt. But there is a more admirable picture described by Mr. Herbert Spencer in his "Study of Sociology," which graphically represents the doctrine of the Trinity in the guise of three persons trying to stand in one pair of boots!

Goethe is cited as a Christian, a believer in the Trinity. Doubtless the Dean forgets his bitter epigram to the effect that he found four things too hard to put up with, and as hateful as poison and serpents; namely, tobacco, garlic, bugs, and the Cross. Heine also is pressed into service, and an excellent prose translation of one of his poems is given, wherein he celebrates the Holy Ghost, the Spirit of God. But Dean Stanley has read his Heine to little purpose if he imagines that this radiant and splendid soldier of progress meant by the Spirit of God the third person of the Christian Trinity. Heine was no Christian, and the very opposite of a theologian. We might translate passages of scathing irony on the ascetic creed of the Cross from the De L'Allemagne, but space does not admit. A few of Heine's last words must do instead. To Adolph Stahr he said: "For the man in good health Christianity is an unserviceable religion, with its resignation and one-sided precepts. For the sick man, however, I assure you it is a very good religion." To Alfred Meissner: "When health is used up, money used up, and sound human sense used up, Christianity begins." Once, while lying on his mattress-grave, he said with a sigh: "If I could even get out on crutches, do you know whither I would go? Straight to church."

And when his hearer looked incredulous, he added: "Most decidedly to church. Where else should one go with crutches?" Such exquisite and mordant irony is strange indeed in a defender of the holy and blessed Trinity.

Dean Stanley's peroration runs thus:—"Wherever we are taught to know and understand the real nature of the world in which our lot is cast, there is a testimony, however humble, to the name of the Father; wherever we are taught to know and admire the highest and best of human excellence, there is a testimony to the name of the Son: wherever there is implanted in us a presence of freedom, purity and love, there is a testimony to the name of the Holy Ghost." Very fine, no doubt; also very soporific. One is inclined to mutter a sleepy Amen. If this passage means anything at all it implies that all who know truth, admire excellence, and have any share in freedom and virtue, are testators to the names of Father, Son and Holy Ghost; so that many Atheists are Trinitarians without knowing it. "In Christianity," says the Dean, "no thing is of real concern except that which makes us wiser and better." That is precisely what the sceptic says, yet for that coroners reject his service on juries, and rowdy Christians try to keep him out of Parliament when he has a legal right to enter. But the Dean adds: "Everything which does make us wiser and better is the very thing which Christianity intends." That is, Christianity means just what you like to find in it. How can a man of Dean Stanley's eminence and ability write such dishonest trash? Must we charitably, though with a touch of sarcasm, repeat Lamb's words of Coleridge—"Never mind; it's only his fun?"

GOD AND THE QUEEN

(March, 1882)

The Queen is now safely lodged at Mentone. Although the political outlook is not very bright, there is pretty sure to be a good solid majority to vote a dowry for Prince Leopold's bride; and so long as royalty is safe it does not much matter what becomes of the people. That dreadful Bradlaugh is gagged; he cannot open his mouth in the House of Commons against perpetual pensions or royal grants. The interests of monarchy are in no immediate peril, and so the Queen is off to Mentone.

Now she is gone, and the loyal hubbub has subsided, it is just the time to consider her late "providential escape" from the bullet which was never fired at her.

What is the meaning of providential? God does all or nothing. There is a special providence in the fall of a sparrow, as well as in the fall of empires. In that case everything is providential. But this is not the ordinary view. When a railway accident occurs those who do not come to grief ascribe their preservation to Providence. Who then is responsible for the fate of those who perish? Centuries ago Christians would have answered, "the Devil." Now they give no answer at all, but treat the question as frivolous or profane.

Thomas Cooper, in his Autobiography, says that the perfecting touch was given to his conversion by an interposition of God. During a collision, the carriage in which he sat was lifted clean on to another line of rails, and thus escaped the fate of the other carriages, which were broken to pieces. Pious Thomas recognised at once the finger of God, and he there and then fell on his knees and offered up a thanksgiving. He was too vain to carry his argument out to its logical end. Why did the Lord protect him, and not his fellow-travellers? Was he of more importance than any of the others? And why, if it was right to thank God for saving Thomas Cooper, would it be wrong to curse him for smashing all the rest?

This superstition of Providence is dying out. Common people are gradually being left to the laws of Nature. If a workhouse were to catch on fire, no one would speak of those who escaped the flames as providentially saved. God does not look after the welfare of paupers; nor is it likely that he would pluck a charwoman's brat out of the fire if it tumbled in during her absence. Such interpositions are absurd. But with kings, queens, princes, princesses, and big nobs in general, the case is different. God looks after the quality. He stretches forth his hand to save them from danger, from the pestilence that walketh by day and the terror that walketh by night. And his worshippers take just the same view of the "swells." When the Queen came to London, a few weeks ago, one of her mounted attendants was thrown and badly hurt; and the next day one of the loyal Tory papers reported that her Majesty had completely recovered from the accident to her outrider!

But if the Lord overlooks the great ones of the earth, why is he not impartial? He did not turn aside Guiteau's bullet, nor did he answer the prayers of a whole nation on its knees. President Garfield was allowed to die after a long agony. Poor Mrs. Garfield believed up to the very last minute that God would interpose and save her husband. But he never did. Why was he so indifferent in this case? Was it because Garfield was a President instead of a King, the elected leader of free men instead of the hereditary ruler of political slaves? Informer Newdegate would say so. In his opinion God

Almighty hates Republicans. Yet the Bible clearly shows that the Lord is opposed to monarchy. He gave his chosen people a king as a punishment, after plainly telling them what an evil they had sought; and there is perhaps a covert irony in the story of Saul, the son of Kish, who went to seek his father's asses and found instead a nation of subjects—two-legged asses, who begged him to mount them and ride.

Take another case. Why did God permit the Nihilists to assassinate the late Czar of Russia? All their previous plots had failed. Why was the last plot allowed to succeed? There is only one answer. God had nothing to do with any of them, and the last succeeded because it was better devised and more carefully executed. If God protected the Czar against their former attempts, they were too many for him in the end; that is, they defeated Omnipotence—an absurdity too flagrant for any sane man to believe.

Why should God care for princes more than for peasants, for queens more than for washerwomen? There is no difference in their compositions; they are all made of the same flesh and blood. The very book these loyal gushers call the Word of God declares that he is no respecter of persons. What are the distinctions of rank and wealth? Mere nothings. Look down from an altitude of a thousand feet, and an emperor and his subjects shall appear equally small; and what are even a thousand feet in the infinite universe? Nay, strip them of all their fictions of dress; reduce them to the same condition of featherless bipeds; and you shall find the forms of strength or beauty, and the power of brain, impartially distributed by Nature, who is the truest democrat, who raises her Shakespeares from the lowest strata of society, and laughs to scorn the pride of palaces and thrones.

Providence is an absurdity, a superstitious relic of the ignorant past.

Sensible men disbelieve it, and scientists laugh it to scorn. Our very moral sense revolts against it. Why should God help a few of his children and neglect all the others? Explosions happen in mines, and scores of honest industrious men, doing the rough work of the world and winning bread for wife and child, are blown to atoms or hurled into shapeless death. God does not help them, and tears moisten the dry bread of half-starved widows and orphans. Sailors on the mighty deep go down with uplifted hands, or slowly gaze their life away on the merciless heavens. The mother bends over her dying child, the first flower of her wedded love, the sweetest hope of her life. She is rigid with despair, and in her hot tearless eyes there dwells a dumb misery that would touch a heart of stone. But God does not help, the death-curtain falls, and darkness reigns where all was light.

Who has the audacity to say that the God who will not aid a mother in the death-chamber shelters the Queen upon her throne? It is an insult to reason and a ghastly mockery of justice. The impartiality of Nature is better than the mercy of such a God.

CARDINAL NEWMAN ON INFIDELITY

(April, 1882)

Cardinal Newman is perhaps the only Catholic in England worth listening to. He has immured his intellect in the catacombs of the Romish Church, but he has not been able to quench it, and even there it radiates a splendor through the gloom. His saintly character is as indubitable as the subtlety of his mind, and no vicissitude has impaired the charm of his style, which is pure and perfect as an exquisite and flawless diamond; serene and chaste in its usual mood, but scintillating gloriously in the light of his imagination.

On Sunday last Cardinal Newman preached a sermon at the Oratory in Birmingham on "Modern Infidelity." Unfortunately we have not a full report, from which we might be able to extract some notable passages, but only a newspaper summary. Even this, however, shows some points of interest.

Cardinal Newman told his hearers that "a great storm of infidelity and irreligion was at hand," and that "some dreadful spiritual catastrophe was coming upon them." We quite agree with the great preacher; but every storm is not an evil, and every catastrophe is not a disaster. The revolutionary storm in France cleared the air of much pestilence. It dissipated as by enchantment the horrible cloud of tyranny, persecution and want, which had for centuries hovered over the land. And certainly, to go back a stage farther in history, the Reformation was not a misfortune, although it looked like a "spiritual catastrophe" to a great many amiable people. The truth is, Revolutions must occur in this world, both in thought and in action.

They may happen slowly, so that we may accommodate ourselves to them; or rapidly, and so disturb and injure whole generations.

But come they must, and no power can hinder them; not even that once mighty Church which has always striven to bind Humanity to the past with adamantine chains of dogma. In Cardinal Newman's own words, from perhaps his greatest and most characteristic book,—"here below to live is to change, and to be perfect is to have changed often."

We cannot say that Cardinal Newman indicates how humanity will suffer from the "coming storm of infidelity and irreligion." He does, indeed, refer to the awful state of a people forsaken by God, but in our humble opinion this is somewhat ludicrous. We can hardly understand how God can forsake his own creatures. Why all this pother if he really exists? In that case our scepticism cannot affect him, any more than a man's blindness obscures the sun. And surely, if Omnipotence desired us all to believe the truth, the means are ready to hand. The God who said, Let there be light, and there was light, could as easily say, Let all men be Christians, and they would be Christians. If God had spoken the universe would be convinced; and the fact that it is not convinced proves, either that he does not exist, or that he purposely keeps silent, and desires that we should mind our own business.

The only tangible evil Cardinal Newman ventures to indicate is the "indignity which at this moment has come over the Holy Father at Rome." He declares, as to the Pope, that "there hardly seems a place in the whole of Europe where he could put his foot." The Catholics are carrying this pretence of a captive Pope a trifle too far. His Holiness must have a tremendous foot if he cannot put it fairly down on the floor of the Vatican. He and his Cardinals really wail over their loss of temporal power. It would be wiser and nobler to reconcile themselves to the inevitable, and to end the nefarious diplomacy by which they are continually striving to recover what is for ever lost. The whole world is aware of the scandalous misrule and the flagrant immorality which, under the government of the Papacy, made the Eternal City a byword and a reproach. Under the secular government, Rome has made wonderful progress. It has better streets, cleaner inhabitants, less fever and filth, and a much smaller army of priests, beggars, and prostitutes. Catholics may rest assured that the bad old times will never return. They may, of course, promise a reformation of manners if the Holy Father's dominion is restored, but the world will not believe them. Reforming the Papacy, as Carlyle grimly said, is like tinkering a rusty old kettle. If you stop up the holes of it with temporary putty, it may hang together for awhile; but "begin to hammer at it, solder it, to what you call mend and rectify it,—it will fall to shreds, as sure as rust is rust; go all into nameless dissolution,—and the fat in the fire will be a thing worth looking at, poor Pope!"

As a sincere Christian (a very rare thing, by the way, in these days), Cardinal Newman is bound to lament the spread of infidelity. He is a keen observer, and his word may be taken for the fact. A stormy time is undoubtedly coming. Old creeds and institutions will have to give an account of themselves, and nothing that cannot stand the test will live. But truth will not suffer. Criticise the multiplication table as much as you please, and twice two will still be four. In the storm and stress of controversy what is true and solid will survive; only the hollow shams of authority and superstition will collapse. Humanity has nothing to fear, however the Churches may groan.

SUNDAY TYRANNY

(May, 1882)

Last Sunday the myriads of Paris turned out to the Chantilly races. The sun shone brilliantly, and all went merry as a marriage bell. Yet there was no drunkenness or disorder; on the contrary, the multitude behaved with such decorum, that one English correspondent said it would not have appeared strange if a bishop had stepped forward in full canonicals to give them his benediction.

Why cannot Englishmen enjoy their Sunday's leisure like the French? Because we are still under the bondage of Puritanism; because our religious dress is nothing but Hebrew Old Clothes; because we follow Moses instead of Jesus; because we believe that man was made for the Sabbath, instead of the Sabbath for man; because, in short, there are in England a lot of sour Christians who play the dog in the manger, and will neither enjoy themselves on Sunday nor let anyone else. They often prate about liberty, but they understand it as the Yankee did, who defined it as the right to do as he pleased and the right to make everybody else do so too.

Let us all be unhappy on Sunday, is the burden of their song. Now, we have no objection to their being miserable, if they desire it, on that or any other day. This is supposed to be a free country; you decide to be wretched and you select your own time for the treat. But you have no right to interfere with your neighbors. This, however, is what the Christians, with their customary "cheek," will insist on doing. They like going to the church and the public-house on Sunday, and those establishments are permitted to open; they have no wish to go elsewhere, and so they keep all other establishments closed. This is mere impudence. Let them go where they choose, and allow the same freedom to other people. Those who advocate a free Sunday ask for no favor; they demand justice. They do not propose to compel any Christian to enter a museum, a library, or an art gallery; they simply claim the right to go in themselves.

The denial of that right is a violation of liberty, which every free man is bound to resent.

This country is said to be civilised. To a certain extent it is, but all our civilisation has been won against Christianity and its brutal laws. Our toiling masses, in factory, mine, shop, and counting-house, have one day of leisure in the week. Rightly considered it is of infinite value. It is a splendid breathing-time. We cast off the storm and stress of life, fling aside the fierce passion of gain, and let the spirit of humanity throb in our pulses and stream from our eyes. Our fellow man is no longer a rival, but a brother. His gain is not our loss. We enrich each other by the noble give-and-take of fellowship, and feel what it really is to live. Yet our Christian legislature tries its utmost to spoil the boon. It cannot prevent us from visiting each other, or walking as far as our legs will carry us; but almost everything else is tabooed. Go to church, it says. Millions answer, We are sick of going; we have heard the same old story until it is unspeakably stale, and many of the sermons have been so frequently repeated that we suspect they were bought by the dozen. Then it says, Go to the public-house. But a huge multitude answer, We don't want to go there either, except for a minute to quench our thirst; we have no wish for spirituous any more than spiritual intoxication; we desire some other alternative than gospel or gin. Then our Christian legislature answers, You are discontented fools. It crushes down their better aspirations, and condemns them to a wearisome inactivity.

Go through London, the metropolis of the world, as we call it, on a Sunday. How utterly dreary it is! The shutters are all up before the gay shop-windows. You pace mile after mile of streets, with sombre houses on either hand as though tenanted by the dead. You stand in front of the British Museum, and it looks as if it had been closed since the date of the mummies inside. You yearn to walk through its galleries, to gaze on the relics of antiquity, to inspect the memorials of the dead, to feel the subtle links that bind together the past and the present and make one great family of countless generations of men. But you must wander away disappointed and dejected. You repair to the National Gallery. You long to behold the masterpieces of art, to have your imagination quickened and thrilled by the glories of form and color, to look once more on some favorite picture which touches your nature to its finest issues. But again you are foiled. You desire to visit a library, full of books you cannot buy, and there commune with the great minds who have left their thoughts to posterity. But you are frustrated again. You are cheated out of your natural right, and treated less like a man than a dog.

This Christian legislature has much to answer for. Drunkenness is our great national vice. And how is it to be overcome? Preaching will not do it. Give Englishmen a chance, furnish them with counter attractions, and they will abjure intoxication like their continental neighbors. Elevate their tastes, and they will feel superior to the vulgar temptation of drink. Every other method has been tried and has failed; this is the only method that promises success.

Fortunately the Sunday question is growing. Christian tyranny is evidently doomed. Mr. Howard's motion for the opening of public museums and art galleries, although defeated, received the support of eighty-five members of Parliament. That minority will increase again next year, and in time it will become a majority. Mr. Broadhurst, for some peculiar reason, voted against it, but we imagine he will some day repent of his action. The working-classes are fools if they listen to the idle talk about Sunday labor, with which the Tories and bigots try to bamboozle them. The opening of public institutions on Sunday would not necessitate a hundredth part of the labor already employed in keeping open places of worship, and driving rich people to and fro. All the nonsense about the thin end of the wedge is simply dust thrown into their eyes. The very people who vote against Sunday freedom under a pretence of opposing Sunday labor, keep their own servants at work and visit the "Zoo" in the afternoon, where they doubtless chuckle over the credulity of the lower orders. Christian tyranny unites with Tory oppression to debase and enslave the people. It is time that both were imperiously stopped. The upper classes wish to keep us ignorant, and parsons naturally want everybody else's shutters up when they open shop. We ought to see through the swindle. Let us check their impudence, laugh at their hypocrisy, and rescue our Sunday from their hands.

WHO ARE THE BLASPHEMERS?

(June, 1882)

Atheists are often charged with blasphemy, but it is a crime they cannot commit. God is to them merely a word, expressing all sorts of ideas, and not a person. It is, properly speaking, a general term, which includes all that there is in common among the various deities of the world. The idea of the supernatural embodies itself in a thousand ways. Truth is always simple and the same, but error is infinitely diverse. Jupiter, Jehovah and Mumbo-Jumbo are alike creations of human fancy, the products of ignorance and wonder. Which is the God is not yet settled. When the sects have decided this point, the question may take a fresh turn; but until then god must be considered as a generic term, like tree or horse or men; with just this difference, however, that while the words tree, horse and man express the general qualities of visible objects, the word god expresses only the imagined qualities of something that nobody has ever seen.

When the Atheist examines, denounces, or satirises the gods, he is not dealing with persons but with ideas. He is incapable of insulting God, for he does not admit the existence of any such being.

Ideas of god may be good or bad, beautiful or ugly; and according as he finds them the Atheist treats them. If we lived in Turkey we should deal with the god of the Koran, but as we live in England we deal with the god of the Bible. We speak of that god as a being, just for convenience sake, and not from conviction. At bottom, we admit nothing but the mass of contradictory notions between Genesis and

Revelation. We attack not a person but a belief, not a being but an idea, not a fact but a fancy.

Lord Brougham long ago pointed out, in his "Life of Voltaire," that the great French heretic was not guilty of blasphemy, as his enemies alleged; since he had no belief in the actual existence of the god he dissected, analysed and laughed at. Mr. Ruskin very eloquently defends Byron from the same charge. In "Cain," and elsewhere, the great poet does not impeach God; he merely impeaches the orthodox creed. We may sum up the whole matter briefly. No man satirises the god he believes in, and no man believes in the god he satirises.

We shall not, therefore, be deterred by the cry of "blasphemy," which is exactly what the Jewish priests shouted against Jesus Christ. If there is a God, he cannot be half so stupid and malignant as the Bible declares. In destroying the counterfeit we do not harm the reality. And as it is better, in the words of Plutarch, to have no notion of the gods than to have notions which dishonor them, we are satisfied that the Lord (if he exist) will never burn us in hell for denying a few lies told in his name.

The real blasphemers are those who believe in God and blacken his character; who credit him with less knowledge than a child, and less intelligence than an idiot; who make him quibble, deceive, and lie; who represent him as indecent, cruel, and revengeful; who give him the heart of a savage and the brain of a fool. These are the blasphemers.

When the priest steps between husband and wife, with the name of God on his lips, he blasphemes. When, in the name of God, he resists education and science, he blasphemes. When, in the name of God, he opposes freedom of thought and liberty of conscience, he blasphemes. When, in the name of God, he robs, tortures, and kills those who differ from him, he blasphemes. When, in the name of God, he opposes the equal rights of all, he blasphemes. When, in the name of God, he preaches content to the poor and oppressed, flatters the rich and powerful, and makes religious tyranny the handmaiden of political privilege, he blasphemes. And when he takes the Bible in his hand, and says it was written by the inspiration of God, he blasphemes almost beyond forgiveness.

Who are the blasphemers? Not we who preach freedom and progress for all men; but those who try to bind the world with chains of dogma, and to burden it, in God's name, with all the foul superstitions of its ignorant past.

THE BIRTH OF CHRIST

(December, 1880)

"The time draws near, the birth of Christ," as Tennyson sings in "In Memoriam," and the pious followers of the Nazarene will celebrate it with wonted orgies of pleasure. The Incarnation will be pondered to the accompaniment of roast beef, and the Atonement will play lambently around the solid richness of plum-pudding. And thus will be illustrated the biological truth that the stomach is the basis of everything, including religion.

But while Christians comport themselves thus in presence of the subtlest mysteries of faith, the Sceptic cannot be without his peculiar reflections. He, of course, knows that the festal observance of this season is far more ancient than Christianity; but he naturally wonders how people, who imagine it to be a unique feature of their sublimely spiritual creed, remain contented with its extremely sensual character. They profess to believe that the fate of the whole human race was decided by the advent of the Man of Sorrows; yet they commemorate that event by an unhealthy consumption of the meat which perisheth, and a wild indulgence in the frivolous pleasures of that carnal mind which is at enmity with God. Astonished at such conduct, the Sceptic muses on the inconsistency of mankind. He may also once more consider the circumstances of the birth of Christ and its relation to the history of the modern world.

Jesus, called the Christ, is popularly supposed to have been of the seed of David, from which it was promised that the Messiah should come. It is, however, perfectly clear that he was in no-wise related to the man after God's own heart His putative father, Joseph, admittedly had no share in bringing him into the world; for he disdained the assistance of a father, although he was unable to dispense with that of a mother. But Joseph, and not Mary, according to the genealogies of Matthew and Luke, was the distant blood relation of David; and therefore Jesus was not of the seed of the royal house, but a bastard slip grafted on the ancient family-tree by the Holy Ghost. It is a great pity that newspaper correspondents did not exist in those days. Had Joseph been skilfully "interviewed," it is highly probable that the world would have been initiated into his domestic secrets, and enlightened as to the paternity of Mary's eldest son. The Holy Ghost is rather too shadowy a personage to be the father of a lusty boy, and no young lady would be credited in this age if she ascribed to him the authorship of a child born out of wedlock. Most assuredly no magistrate would make an order against him for its maintenance. Even a father of the Spiritualist persuasion, who believed in what is grandly called "the materialisation of spirit forms," would probably be more than dubious if his daughter were to present him with a grandson whose father lived on the other side of death and resided in a mansion not made with hands. It is, we repeat, to be for ever regretted that poor Joseph has not left his version of the affair. The Immaculate Conception might perhaps have been cleared up, and theology relieved of a half-obscene mystery, which has unfortunately perverted not a few minds.

The birth of Jesus was announced to "wise men from the East" by the appearance of a singular star. Is not this a relic of astrology? Well does Byron sing—

"Ye stars! which are the poetry of heaven,
If in your bright beams we would read the fate

> *Of men and empires, 'tis to be forgiven,*
> *That in our aspirations to be great*
> *Our destinies o'erleap their mortal state,*
> *And claim a kindred with you; for ye are*
> *A beauty and a mystery, and create*
> *In us such love and reverence from afar*
> *That fortune, fame, power, life,*
> *Have named themselves a star."*

But this star was the most wonderful on record. It "went before" the wise men, and "stood over where the young child was." Such an absurdity could be related and credited only by people who conceived of the sky as a solid vault, not far distant, wherein all the heavenly bodies were stuck. The present writer once asked an exceedingly ignorant and simple man where he thought he would alight if he dropped from the comet then in the sky. "Oh," said he, naming the open space nearest his own residence, "somewhere about Finsbury Circus." That man's astronomical notions were very imperfect, but they were quite as good as those of the person who seriously wrote, and of the persons who seriously believe, this fairy tale of the star which heralded the birth of Christ.

Luke's version of the episode differs widely from Matthew's. He makes no reference to "wise men from the East," but simply says that certain "shepherds" of the same country, who kept watch over their flock by night, were visited by "the angel of the Lord," and told that they would find the Savior, Christ the Lord, just born at Bethlehem, the City of David, "wrapped in swaddling clothes and lying in a manger." Luke does not, as is generally supposed, represent Mary as confined in a stable because Joseph was too poor to pay for decent accommodation, but because "there was no room for them in the inn." It is perfectly consistent with all the Gospel references to Joseph's status to assume that he carried on a flourishing business, and Jesus himself in later years might doubtless have earned a good living in the concern if he had not deliberately preferred to lead the life of a mendicant preacher. This, however, is by the way. Our point is that Luke says nothing about the "star" or the "wise men from the East," who had an important interview with Herod himself; while Matthew says nothing about the "manger" or the shepherds and their angelic visitors. Surely these discrepancies on points so important, and as to which there could be little mistake, are enough to throw discredit on the whole story.

It is further noticeable that Luke is absolutely silent about Herod's massacre of the innocents. What can we think of his reticence on such a subject? Had the massacre occurred, it would have been widely known, and the memory of so horrible a deed would have been vivid for generations. Matthew, or whoever wrote the Gospel which bears his name, is open to suspicion. His mind was distorted by an intense belief in prophecy, a subject which, as old Bishop South said, either finds a man cracked or leaves him so. After narrating the story of Herod's massacre, he adds: "Then was fulfilled that which was spoken by Jeremy, the prophet, saying," etc. Now, he makes similar reference to prophecy no less than five times in the first two chapters, and in each case we find that the "prophetical" utterance referred to has not the faintest connexion with the incident related.

Besides, a man who writes history with one eye on his own period, and the other on a period centuries anterior is not likely to be veracious, however earnestly he may intend to. There is an early tradition, which is as strong as any statement about the history of the Primitive Church, that Matthew's Gospel was originally written in Hebrew; and it has been supposed that the writer gratuitously threw in these references to Jeremy and others, in order to please the Jews, who were extremely fond of prophecy. But this supposition is equally fatal to his credibility as an historian. In any case, the Evangelists differ so widely on matters of such interest and importance that we are constrained to discredit their story. It is evidently, as scholarship reveals, a fairy tale, which slowly gathered round the memory of Jesus after his death. Some of its elements were creations of his disciples' fancy, but others were borrowed from the mythology of more ancient creeds.

Yet this fairy tale is accepted by hundreds of millions of men as veritable history. It is incorporated into the foundation of Christianity, and every year at this season its incidents are joyously commemorated. How slowly the world of intelligence moves! But let us not despair. Science and scholarship have already done much to sap belief in this supernatural religion, and we may trust them to do still more. They will ultimately destroy its authority by refuting its pretensions, and compel it to take its place among the general multitude of historic faiths.

If Jesus was the Christ, the Messiah, the Deliverer, why is the world still so full of sin and misery? The Redeemer has come, say the Christians. Yes, we reply, but when will come the redemption? Apostrophising Jesus in his lines "Before a Crucifix," Mr. Swinburne reminds him that "the nineteenth wave of the ages rolls now usward since thy birth began," and then inquires:—

> "Hast thou fed full men's starved-out souls,
> Or are there less oppressions done
> In this wide world under the sun?"

Only a negative answer can be given. Christ has in no wise

redeemed the world. He was no god of power, but a weak fallible man like ourselves; and his cry of despair on the cross might now be repeated with tenfold force. The older myth of Prometheus is truer and more inspiring than the myth of Christ. If there be gods, they have never yielded man aught of their grace. All his possessions have been cunningly, patiently, and valorously extorted from the powers that be, even as Prometheus filched the fire from heaven. In that realm of mythology, whereto all religions will eventually be consigned, Jesus will dwindle beneath Prometheus. One is feminine, and typifies resigned submission to a supernatural will; the other is masculine, and typifies that insurgent audacity of heart and head, which has wrested a kingdom of science from the vast empire of nescience, and strewed the world with the wrecks of theological power.

THE REIGN OF CHRIST

(January, 1880)

Christmas and Easter are fruitful in panegyrics on Jesus and the religion which fraudulently bears his name. On these occasions, not only the religious but even the secular newspapers give the rein to their rhetoric and imagination, and indulge in much fervid eloquence on the birth or the crucifixion of the Nazarene. Time-honored platitudes are brought out from their resting-places and dexterously moved to a well-known tune; and fallacies which have been refuted ad nauseam are paraded afresh as though their logical purity were still beyond suspicion. Papers that differ on all other occasions and on all other subjects concur then, and "when they do agree their unanimity is wonderful." While the more sober and orthodox discourse in tones befitting their dignity and repute, the more profane riotously join in the chorus; and not to be behind the rest, the notoriously misbelieving Greatest Circulator orders from the profanest member of its staff "a rousing article on the Crucifixion," or on the birth of Jesus, as the case may be. All this, however, is of small account, except as an indication of the slavery of our "independent" journals to Bumble and his prejudices, before whom they are obliged to masquerade when he ordains a celebration of his social or religious rites. But here and there a more serious voice is heard through the din, with an accent of earnest veracity, and not that of an actor playing a part. Such a voice may be worth listening to, and certainly no other can be. Let us hear the Rev. J. Baldwin Brown on "The Reign of Christ." He is, I believe, honorably distinguished among Dissenters; his sermons often bear marks of originality; and the goodness of his heart, whatever may be thought of the strength of his head, is sufficiently attested by his emphatic revolt against the doctrine of Eternal Torture in Hell.

Before criticising Mr. Brown's sermon in detail I cannot help remarking that it is far too rhetorical and far too empty of argument. Sentimentality is the bane of religion in our day; subservience to popularity degrades the pulpit as it degrades the press. If we desire to find the language of reason in theology, we must seek it in the writings of such men as Newman, who contemplate the ignorant and passionate multitude with mingled pity and disdain. The "advanced" school of theologians, from Dean Stanley to the humblest reconciler of reason and faith, are sentimentalists almost to a man; the reason being, I take it, that although their emotional tendencies are very admirable, they lack the intellectual consistency and rigor which impel others to stand on definite first principles, as a sure basis of operation and an impregnable citadel against attack. Mr. Brown belongs to this "advanced" school, and has a liberal share of its failings. He is full of eloquent passages that lead to nothing, and he excites expectations which are seldom if ever satisfied. He faces stupendous obstacles raised by reason against his creed, and just as we look to see him valiantly surmount them, we find that he veils them from base to summit with a dense cloud of words, out of which his voice is heard asking us to believe him on the other side. Yet of all men professional students of the Bible should be freest from such a fault, seeing what a magnificent masterpiece it is of terse and vigorous simplicity. Mr. Brown and his "advanced" friends would do well to ponder that quaint and pregnant aphorism of old Bishop Andrewes—"Waste words addle questions." When I first read it I was thrown into convulsions of laughter, and even now it tickles my risibility; but despite its irresistible quaint-ness I cannot but regard it as one of the wisest and pithiest sentences in our literature. Dr. Newman has splendidly amplified it in a passage of his "University Sermons," which I gratuitously present to Mr. Brown and every reader who can make use of it:—"Half the controversies in the world are verbal ones; and could they be brought to a plain issue, they would be brought to a prompt termination. Parties engaged in them would then perceive, either that in substance they agreed together, or that their difference was one of first principles. This is the great object to be aimed at in the present age, though confessedly a very arduous one. We need not dispute, we need not prove,—we need but define. At all events, let us, if we can, do this first of all; and then see who are left for us to dispute with, and what is left for us to prove."

Mr. Brown's sermon on "The Reign of Christ" is preached from a verse of St. Paul's first Epistle to Timothy, wherein Jesus is styled "The blessed and only Potentate." From this "inspired" statement he derives infinite consolation. This, he admits, is far from being the best of all possible worlds, for it is full of strife and cruelty, the wail of anguish and the clamor of frenzy; but as Christ is "the blessed and only Potentate," moral order will finally be evolved from the chaos and good be triumphant over evil. Now the question arises: Who made the chaos and who is responsible for the evil? Not Christ, of course: Mr. Brown will not allow that. Is it the Devil then? Oh no! To say that would be blasphemy against God. He admits, however, that the notion has largely prevailed, and has even been formulated into religious creeds, "that a malignant spirit, a spirit who loves cursing as God loves blessing, has a large and independent share in the government of the world." But, he adds, "in Christendom men dare not say that they believe it, with the throne of the crucified and risen Christ revealed in the Apocalypse to their gaze." Ordinary people will rub their eyes in sheer amazement at this cool assertion. Is it not plain that Christians in all ages have believed in the power and subtlety of the Devil as God's sleepless antagonist? Have they not held, and do they not still hold, that he caused the Fall of Adam and Eve, and thus introduced original sin, which was certain to infect the whole human race ever afterwards until the end of time? Was not John Milton a Christian, and did he not in his "Paradise Lost" develope all the phases of that portentous competition between the celestial and infernal powers for the virtual possession of this world and lordship over the destinies of our race? If we accept Mr. Brown's statements we shall have to reverse history and belie the evidence of our senses.

But who is responsible for the moral chaos and the existence of evil? That is the question. If to say Christ is absurd, and to say the Devil blasphemy, what alternative is left? The usual answer is: Man's freewill. Christ as "the blessed and only Potentate" leaves us liberty of action, and our own evil passions cause all the misery of our lives. But who gave us our evil passions? To this question no answer is vouchsafed, and so we are left exactly at the point from which we started. Yet Mr. Brown has a very decided opinion as to the part these "evil passions" play in the history cf mankind. He refers to them as "the Devil's brood of lust and lies, and wrongs and hates, and murderous passion and insolent power, which through all the ages of earth's sad history have made it liker hell than heaven." No Atheist could use stronger language. Mr. Brown even believes that our "insurgent lusts and passions" are predetermining causes of heresy, so that in respect both to faith and to works they achieve our damnation. How then did we come by them? The Evolutionist frankly answers the question without fear of blasphemy on the one hand or of moral despair on the other. Mr.

Brown is bound to give his answer after raising the question so vividly. But he will not. He urges that it "presents points of tremendous difficulty," although "we shall unravel the mystery, we shall solve the problems in God's good time." Thus the solution of the problem is to be postponed until we are dead, when it will no longer interest us. However convenient this may be for the teachers of mystery, it is most unsatisfactory to rationalists. Mr. Brown must also be reminded that the "tremendous difficulties" he alludes to are all of his own creation. There is no difficulty about any fact except in relation to some theory. It is Mr. Brown's theory of the universe which creates the difficulties. It does not account for all the facts of existence—nay, it is logically contravened by the most conspicuous and persistent of them. Instead of modifying or transforming his theory into accordance with the facts, he rushes off with it into the cloud-land of faith. There let him remain as he has a perfect right to. Our objection is neither to reason nor to faith, but to a mischievous playing fast and loose with both.

Mr. Brown opines that Christ will reign until all his enemies are under his feet. And who are these enemies? Not the souls of men, says Mr. Brown, for Christ "loves them with an infinite tenderness." This infinite tenderness is clearly not allied to infinite power or the world's anguish would long since have been appeased and extinguished, or never have been permitted to exist at all. The real enemies of Christ are not the souls of men, but "the hates and passions which torment them." Oh those hates and passions! They are the dialectical balls with which Mr. Brown goes through his performance in that circle of petitio principii so hated by all logicians, the middle sphere of intellects too light for the solid earth of fact and too gross for the aerial heaven of imagination.

It will be a fitting conclusion to present to Mr. Brown a very serious matter which he has overlooked. Christ, "the blessed and only Potentate," came on earth and originated the universal religion nearly two thousand years ago. Up to the present time three-fourths of the world's inhabitants are outside its pale, and more than half of them have never heard it preached. Amongst the quarter which nominally professes Christianity disbelief is spreading more rapidly than the missionaries succeed in converting the heathen; so that the reign of Christ is being restricted instead of increased. To ask us, despite this, to believe that he is God, and possessed of infinite power, is to ask us to believe a marvel compared with which the wildest fables are credible, and the most extravagant miracles but as dust in the balance.

THE PRIMATE ON MODERN INFIDELITY

(September, 1880)

A bishop once twitted a curate with preaching indifferent orthodoxy. "Well," answered the latter, "I don't see how you can expect me to be as orthodox as yourself. I believe at the rate of a hundred a year, and you at the rate of ten thousand." In the spirit of this anecdote we should expect an archbishop to be as orthodox as the frailty of human nature will allow. A man who faithfully believes at the rate of fifteen thousand a year should be able to swallow most things and stick at very little. And there can be no doubt that the canny Scotchman who has climbed or wriggled up to the Archbishopric of Canterbury is prepared to go any lengths his salary may require. We suspect that he regards the doctrines of the Church very much as did that irreverent youth mentioned by Sidney Smith, who, on being asked to sign the Thirty-nine Articles, replied "Oh yes, forty if you like." The clean linen of his theology is immaculately pure. Never has he fallen under a suspicion of entertaining dangerous or questionable opinions, and he has in a remarkable degree that faculty praised by Saint Paul of being all things to all men, or at least as many men as make a lumping majority. What else could be expected from a Scotchman who has mounted to the spiritual Primacy of England?

His Grace has recently been visiting the clergy and churchwardens of his diocese and delivering what are called Charges to them. The third of these was on the momentous subject of Modern Infidelity, which seems to have greatly exercised his mind. This horrid influence is found to be very prevalent, much to the disconcertion of his Grace, who felt constrained to begin his Charge with expressions of despondency, and only recovered his spirits towards the end, where he confidently relies on the gracious promise of Christ never to forsake his darling church. Some of the admissions he makes are worth recording—

"I can," he says, "have no doubt that the aspect of Christian society in the present day is somewhat troubled, that the Church of Christ and the faith of Christ are passing through a great trial in all regions of the civilised world, and not least among ourselves. There are dark clouds on the horizon already breaking, which may speedily burst into a violent storm.... It is well to note in history how these two evils—superstition and infidelity—act and react in strengthening each other. Still, I cannot doubt that the most [? more] formidable of the two for us at present is infidelity.... It is indeed a frightful thought that numbers of our intelligent mechanics seem to be alienated from all religious ordinances, that our Secularist halls are well filled, that there is an active propagandism at work for shaking belief in all creeds."

These facts are of course patent, but it is something to get an Archbishop to acknowledge them, His Grace also finds "from above, in the regions of literature and art, efforts to degrade mankind by denying our high original:" the high original being, we presume, a certain simple pair called Adam and Eve, who damned themselves and nearly the whole of their posterity by eating an apple six thousand years ago. The degradation of a denial of this theory is hardly perceptible to untheological eyes. Most candid minds would prefer to believe in Darwin rather than in Moses even if the latter had, which he has not, a single leg to stand on. For the theory of our Simian origin at least involves progression in the past and perhaps salvation in the future of our race, while the "high original" theory involved our retrogression and perdition. His grace wonders how these persons can "confine their hopes and aspirations to a life which is so irresistibly hastening to its speedy conclusion." But surely he is aware that they do so for the very simple reason that they know nothing of any other life to hope about or aspire to. One bird in the hand is worth twenty in the bush when the bush itself remains obstinately invisible, and if properly cooked is worth all the dishes in the world filled only with expectations. His grace likewise refers to the unequal distribution of worldly goods, to the poverty and misery which exist "notwithstanding all attempts to regenerate society by specious schemes of socialistic reorganisation." It is, of course, very natural that an archbishop in the enjoyment of a vast income should stigmatise these "specious schemes" for distributing more equitably the good things of this world; but the words "blessed be ye poor" go ill to the tune of fifteen thousand a year, and there is a grim irony in the fact that palaces are tenanted by men who profess to represent and preach the gospel of him who had not where to lay his head. Modern Christianity has been called a civilised heathenism; with no less justice it might be called an organised hypocrisy.

After a dolorous complaint as to the magazines "lying everywhere for the use of our sons and daughters," in which the doctrines both of natural and of revealed religion are assailed, the Archbishop proceeds to deal with the first great form of infidelity, namely Agnosticism. With a feeble attempt at wit he remarks that the name itself implies a confession of ignorance, which he marvels to find unaccompanied by "the logical result of a philosophical humility." A fair account of the Agnostic position is then given, after which it is severely observed that "the better feelings of man contradict these sophisms." In proof of this, his Grace cites the fact that in Paris, the "stronghold of Atheistical philosophy," the number of burials that take place without religious rites is "a scarcely appreciable percentage." We suspect the accuracy of this statement, but having no statistics on the subject by us, we are not prepared to dispute it. We will assume its truth; but the important question then arises— What kind of persons are those who dispense with the rites of religion? Notoriously they are men of the highest intellect and character, whose quality far outweighs the quantity of the other side. They are the leaders of action and thought, and what they think and do to-day will be thought and done by the masses to-morrow. When a man like Gambetta, occupying such a high position and wielding such immense influence, invariably declines to enter a church, whether he attends the marriage or the funeral of his friends, we are entitled to say that his example on our side is infinitely more important than the practice of millions who are creatures of habit and for the most part blind followers of tradition. The Archbishop's argument tells against his own position, and the fact he cites, when closely examined, proves more for our side than he thought it proved for his own.

Atheism is disrelished by his Grace even more than Agnosticism. His favorite epithet for it is "dogmatic." "Surely," he cries, "the boasted enlightenment of this century will never tolerate the gross ignorance and arrogant self-conceit which presumes to dogmatise as to things confessedly beyond its ken." Quite so; but that is what the theologians are perpetually doing. To use Matthew Arnold's happy expression, they talk familiarly about God as though he were a man living in the next street. The Atheist and the Agnostic confess their inability to fathom the universe and profess doubts as to the ability of others. Yet they are called dogmatic, arrogant, and self-conceited. On the other hand, the theologians claim the power of seeing through nature up to nature's God. Yet they, forsooth, must be accounted modest, humble, and retiring.

> *"O wad some pow'r the giftie gie us*
> *To see oursels as ithers see us!"*

These abominable Atheists are by no means scarce, for, says his Grace, "practical Atheists we have everywhere, if Atheism be the denial of God." Just so; that is precisely what we "infidels" have been saying for years. Christianity is utterly alien to the life of modern society, and in flagrant contradiction to the spirit of our secular progress. It stands outside all the institutions of our material civilisation. Its churches still echo the old strains of music and the old dogmatic tones from the pulpit, but the worshippers themselves feel the anomaly of its doctrines and rites when they return to their secular avocations. The Sunday does nothing but break the continuity of their lives, steeping them in sentiments and ideas which have no relation to their experience during the rest of the week. The profession of Christendom is one thing, its practice is another. God is simply acknowledged with the lips on Sunday, and on every other day profoundly disregarded in all the pursuits of life whether of business or of pleasure. Even in our national legislature, although the practice of prayer is still retained, any man would be sneered at as a fool who made the least appeal to the sanctions of theology. An allusion to the Sermon on the Mount would provoke a smile, and a citation of one of the Thirty-nine Articles be instantly ruled as irrelevant. Nothing from the top to the bottom of our political and social life is done with any reference to those theological doctrines which the nation professes to believe, and to the maintenance of which it devotes annually so many millions of its wealth.

In order to pose any member of the two great divisions of "infidelity," the Archbishop advises his clergy to ask the following rather comical questions:—

"Do you believe nothing which is not capable of being tested by the ordinary rules which govern experience in things natural? How then do you know that you yourself exist? How do you know that the perceptions of your senses are not mere delusions, and that there is anything outside you answering to what your mind conceives? Have you a mind? and if you have not, what is it that enables you to think and reason, and fear, and hope? Are these conditions of your being the mere results of your material organism, like the headache which springs from indigestion, or the high spirits engendered by too much wine? Are you something better than a vegetable highly cultivated, or than your brothers of the lower animals? and, if so, what is it that differentiates your superiority? Why do things outside you obey your will? Who gave you a will? and, if so, what is it? I think you must allow that intellect is a thing almost divine, if there be anything divine; and I think also you must allow that it is not a thing to be propagated as we propagate well-made and high-bred cattle. Whence came Alexander the Great? Whence Charlemagne? And whence the First Napoleon? Was it through a mere process of spontaneous generation that they sprang up to alter by their genius and overwhelming will the destinies of the world? Whence came Homer, Shakespeare, Bacon? Whence came all the great historians? Whence came Plato and all the bright lights of divine philosophy, of divinity, of poetry? Their influence, after all, you must allow to be quite as wide and enduring as any produced by the masters of those positive material sciences which you worship. Do you think that all these great minds—for they are minds, and their work was not the product of a merely highly organised material frame—were the outcome of some system of material generation, which your so-called science can subject to rule, and teach men how to produce by growth, as they grow vegetables?"

The Archbishop is not a very skilful physician. His prescription shows that he has not diagnosed the disease. These strange questions might strike the infidel "all of a heap," as the expressive vernacular has it, but although they might dumbfounder him, they would assuredly not convince. If the Archbishop of Canterbury were not so exalted a personage we should venture to remark that to ask a man how he knows that he exists betrays a marvellous depth of ignorance or folly. Ultimate facts of consciousness are not subjects of proof or disproof; they are their own warranty and cannot be transcended. There is, besides, something extraordinary in an archbishop of the church to which Berkeley belonged supposing that extreme idealism follows only the rejection of deity. Whether the senses are after all delusory does not matter to the Atheist a straw; they are real enough to him, they make his world in which he lives and moves, and it is of no practical consequence whether they mirror an outer world or not. What differentiates you from the lower animals? asks his Grace. The answer is simple—a higher development of nervous structure. Who gave you a will? is just as sensible a question as Who gave you a nose? We have every reason to believe that both can be accounted for on natural grounds without introducing a supernatural donor. The question whether Alexander, Napoleon, Homer, Bacon and Shakespeare came through a process of spontaneous generation is excruciatingly ludicrous. That process could only produce the very lowest form of organism, and not a wonderfully complex being like man who is the product of an incalculable evolution. But the Archbishop did not perhaps intend this; it may be that in his haste to silence the "infidel" he stumbled over his own meaning. Lastly, there is a remarkable naïveté in the aside of the final question—"for they are minds." He should have added "you know," and then the episode would have been delightfully complete. The assumption of the whole point at issue in an innocent parenthesis is perhaps to be expected from a pulpiteer, but it is not likely that the "infidel" will be caught by such a simple stratagem. All these questions are so irrelevant and absurd that we doubt whether his Grace would have the courage to put one of them to any sceptic across a table, or indeed from any place in the world except the pulpit, which is beyond all risk of attack, and whence a man may ask any number of questions without the least fear of hearing one of them answered.

The invitation given by his grace, to "descend to the harder ground of strictest logical argumentation," is very appropriate. Whether the movement be ascending or descending, there is undoubtedly a vast distance between logical argumentation and anything he has yet advanced. But even on the "harder" ground the Archbishop treads no more firmly. He demands to know how the original protoplasm became endowed with life, and if that question cannot be answered he calls upon us to admit his theory of divine agency, as though that made the subject more intelligible. Supernatural hypotheses are but refuges of ignorance. Earl Beaconsfield, in his impish way, once remarked that where knowledge ended religion began, and the Archbishop of Canterbury seems to share that opinion. His Grace also avers that "no one has ever yet been able to refute the argument necessitating a great First Cause." It is very easy to assert this, but rather difficult to maintain it. One assertion is as good as another, and we shall therefore content ourselves with saying that in our opinion the argument for a great First Cause was (to mention only one name) completely demolished by John Stuart Mill, who showed it to be based on a total misconception of the nature of cause and effect, which apply only to phænomenal changes and not to the apparently unchangeable matter and force of which the universe is composed.

But the overwhelming last argument is that "man has something in him which speaks of God, of something above this fleeting world, and rules of right and wrong have their foundation elsewhere than in man's opinion.... that there is an immutable, eternal distinction between right and wrong—that there is a God who is on the side of right." Again we must complain of unbounded assertion. Every point of this rhetorical flourish is disputed by "infidels" who are not likely to yield to anything short of proof. If God is on the side of right he is singularly incapable of maintaining it; for, in this world at least, according to some penetrating minds, the devil has hitherto had it pretty much his own way, and good men have had to struggle very hard to make things even as equitable as we find them. But after all, says his Grace, the supreme defence of the Church against the assaults of infidelity is Christ himself. Weak in argument, the clergy must throw themselves behind his shield and trust in him. Before his brightness "the mists which rise from a gross materialistic Atheism evaporate, and are scattered like the clouds of night before the dawn." It is useless to oppose reason to such preaching as this. We shall therefore simply retort the Archbishop's epithets. Gross and materialistic are just the terms to describe a religion which traffics in blood and declares that without the shedding of it there is no remission of sin; whose ascetic doctrines malign our purest affections and defile the sweetest fountains of our spiritual health; whose heaven is nothing but an exaggerated jeweller's shop, and its hell a den of torture in which God punishes his children for the consequences of his own ignorance, incapacity or crime.

BAITING A BISHOP

(February, 1880)

Bishops should speak as men having authority, and not as the Scribes and Pharisees. Even the smallest of them should be a great man. An archbishop, with fifteen thousand a year, ought to possess a transcendent intellect, almost beyond comprehension; while the worst paid of all the reverend fathers of the Church, with less than a fifth of that salary, ought to possess no common powers of mind. The Bishop of Carlisle is not rich as bishops go, but he enjoys a yearly income of £4,500, besides the patronage of forty-nine livings. Now this quite equals the salary of the Prime Minister of the greatest empire in the world, and the Bishop of Carlisle should therefore be a truly great man. We regret however, to say that he is very much the reverse, if we may judge from a newspaper report which has reached us of his lecture on "Man's Place in Nature," recently delivered before the Keswick Scientific and Literary Society. Newspaper reports, we know, are often misleading in consequence of their summary character; nevertheless two columns of small type must give some idea of a discourse, however abstruse or profound; here and there, if such occured, a fine thought or a shrewd observation would shine through the densest veil. Yet, unless our vision be exceptionally obtuse, nothing of the kind is apparent in this report of the Bishop's lecture. Being, as his lordship confessed, the development of "a sermon delivered to the men at the Royal Agricultural Society's Show last summer," the lecture was perhaps, like the sermon, adapted to the bucolic mind, and thus does meagre justice to the genius of its author. His lordship, however, chose to read it before a society with some pretentions to culture, and therefore such a plea cannot avail. As the case stands, we are constrained to accuse the bishop of having delivered a lecture on a question of supreme importance, which would do little credit to the president of a Young Men's Christian Association; and when we reflect that a parson occupied the chair at the meeting, and that the vote of thanks to the episcopal lecturer was moved by a canon, who coupled with it some highly complimentary remarks, we are obliged to think the Church more short of brains than even we had previously believed, and that Mene, Mene, Tekel, Upharsin has already been written on its temple walls by the finger of doom.

Very early in his lecture the Bishop observed that "the Scriptures are built on the hypothesis of the supreme and unique position of man." Well, there is nothing novel in this statement. What we want is some proof of the hypothesis. His lordship's way of supplying this need is, to say the least, peculiar. After saying that "he would rather trust the poet as an exponent of man than he would a student of natural history," he proceeds to quote from Shakespeare, Pope and Plato, and ends that part of his argument with a rhetorical flourish, as though he had thus really settled the whole case of Darwin versus Moses. Our reverence of great poets is probably as deep and sincere as the Bishop's, but we never thought of treating them as scientific authorities, or as witnesses to events that happened hundreds of thousands of years before their birth. Poets deal with subjective facts of consciousness, or with objective facts as related to these. The dry light of the intellect, radiated from the cloudless sun of truth, is not their proper element, but belongs exclusively to the man of science. They move in a softer element suffused with emotion, whose varied clouds are by the sun of imagination touched to all forms of beauty and splendor. The scientific man's description of a lion, for instance, would be very different from a poet's; because the one would describe the lion as it is in itself, and the other as it affects us, a living whole, through our organs of sight and sound. Both are true, because each is faithful to its purpose and expresses a fact; yet neither can stand for the other, because they express different facts and are faithful to different purposes. Shakespeare poetically speaks of "the ruddy drops that visit this sad heart," but the scientific truth of the circulation of the blood had to await its Harvey. In like manner, it was not Milton but Newton who expounded the Cosmos; the great poet, like Dante before him, wove pre-existent cosmical ideas into the texture of his sublime epic, while the great scientist wove all the truth of them into the texture of his sublime theory. Let each receive his meed of reverent praise, but do not let us appeal to Newton on poetry or to Milton on physics. And when a Bishop of Carlisle, or other diocese, complains that "the views advanced by scientific men tend painfully to degrade the views of poets and philosophers," let us reply that in almost every case the great truths of science have been found to transcend infinitely the marvels of theology, and that the magnificence of song persists through all fluctuations of knowledge, because its real cause lies less in the subject than in the native grandeur of the poet's mind.

Man's place in nature is, indeed, a great question, and it can be settled only by a wide appeal to past and present facts. And those facts, besides being objective realities, must be treated in a purely scientific, and not in a poetic or didactic spirit. Let the poet sing the beauty of a consummate flower; and, if such things are required, let the moralist preach its lessons. But neither should arrogate the prerogative of the botanist, whose special function it is to inform us of its genesis and development, and its true relations to other forms of vegetable life. So with man. The poet may celebrate his passions and aspirations, his joys and sorrows, his laughter and tears, and ever body forth anew the shapes of things unseen; the moralist may employ every fact of his life to illustrate its laws or to enforce its duties; but they must leave it to the biologist to explain his position in the animal economy, and the stages by which it has been reached. With regard to that, Darwin is authoritative, while Moses is not even entitled to a hearing.

Although the Bishop is very ready to quote from the poets, he is not always ready to use them fairly. For instance, he cites the splendid and famous passage in "Hamlet:"—"What a piece of work is man! How noble in reason! How infinite in faculties! in form and moving, how express and admirable! in action, how like an angel! in apprehension, how like a god! the beauty of the world! the paragon of animals!" There his lordship stops, and then exclaims, "Shakespeare knew nothing of the evolution of man from inferior forms." But why did he not continue the quotation? Hamlet goes on to say, "And yet, what to me is this quintessence of dust?" How now, your lordship? We have you on the hip! "Quintessence of dust" comes perilously near to evolution. Does not your lordship remember, too, Hamlet's pursuing the dust of Cæsar to the ignominious bunghole? And have you never reflected how the prescient mind of Shakespeare created an entirely new and wonderful figure in literature, the half-human, half-bestial Caliban, with his god Setebos—a truly marvellous resuscitation of primitive man, that in our day has inspired Mr. Browning's "Caliban on Setebos," which contains the entire essence of all that Tylor and other investigators in the same field have since written on the subject of Animism? It seems that the Lord Bishop of Carlisle reads even the poets to small purpose.

Haughtily waving the biologists aside, his lordship proceeds to remark that "man's superiority is not the same that a dog would claim over a lobster, or an eagle over a worm;" the difference between man and other animals being "not one of degree, but of kind." Such a statement, without the least evidence being adduced to support it, places the Bishop almost outside the pale of civil discussion. When will these lordly ecclesiastics learn that the time for dogmatic assertion is past, and that the intellectual temper of the present age can be satisfied only by proof? We defy the Bishop of Carlisle to indicate a single phase of man's nature which has no parallel in the lower animals. Man's physical structure is notoriously akin to theirs, and even his brain does not imply a distinction of kind, for every convolution of the brain of man is reproduced in the brain of the higher apes. His lordship draws a distinction between instinct and reason, which is purely fanciful and evinces great ignorance of the subject. That, however, is a question we have at present no room to discuss; nor, indeed, is there any necessity to do so, since his lordship presently admits that the lower animals share our "reason" to some extent, just as to a much larger extent we share their "instinct," and thus evacuates the logical fortress he took such pains to construct.

Quitting that ground, which proves too slippery for his feet, the Bishop goes on to notice the moral and aesthetic difference between man and the lower animals. No animal, says his lordship, shows "anything approaching to a love of art." Now we are quite aware that no animal except man ever painted a picture or chiselled a statue, for these things involve a very high development of the artistic faculty. But the appreciation of form and color, which is the foundation of all fine art, is certainly manifested by the lower animals, and by some fathem to an extreme degree. If his lordship doubts this, let him study the ways of animals for himself; or, if he cannot do that, let him read the chapters in Mr. Darwin's "Descent of Man" on sexual selection among birds. If he retains any doubt after that, we must conclude that his head is too hard or too soft to be influenced, in either of which cases he is much to be pitied.

His lordship thinks that the moral sense is entirely absent in the lower animals. This, however, is absurdly untrue; so much so, indeed, that we shall not trouble to refute it Good and noble, he avers, are epithets inapplicable to animals, even to the horse or dog. What vain creatures men are to talk thus! Does his lordship remember Byron's epitaph on his Newfoundland dog, and the very uncomplimentary distinction drawn therein between dogs and men? Look at that big pet with the lordly yet tender eye! How he submits to the boisterous caresses of children, because he knows their weakness and shares their spirit of play! Let their elders do the same, and he will at once show resentment. See him peril his life ungrudgingly for those he loves, or even for comparative strangers! And shall we deny him the epithet of noble or good? Whatever theologians may say, the sound heart of common men and women will answer No!

Lastly, we are told that "the religious sentiment is characteristically and supremely human." But here again we must complain of his lordship's mental confusion. The religious sentiment is not a simple but a highly complex emotion. Resolve it into its elemental feelings, and it will be found that all these are possessed in some degree by lower animals. The feeling of a dog who bays the moon is probably very similar to that of the savage who cowers and moans beneath an eclipse; and if the savage has superstitious ideas as well as awesome feelings, it is only because he possesses a higher development of thought and imagination.

Canon Battersby, who moved the vote of thanks to the Bishop, ridiculed the biologists, and likened them to Topsy who accounted for her existence by saying "Specs I growed." Just so. That is precisely how we all did come into existence. Growth and not making is the law for man as well as for every other form of life. Moses stands for manufacture and Darwin stands for growth. And if the great biologist finds himself in the company of Topsy, he will not mind. Perhaps, indeed, as he is said to enjoy a joke and to be able to crack one, might he jocularly observe to "tremendous personages" like the Bishop of Carlisle, that this is not the first instance of truths being hidden from the "wise" and revealed unto babes.

PROFESSOR FLINT ON ATHEISM

(January, 1877)

Professor Flint delivered last week the first of the present year's course of Baird lectures to a numerous audience in Blythswood Church, Glasgow, taking for his subject "The Theories opposed to Theism." Anti-Theism, he said, is more general now than Atheism, and includes all systems opposed to Theism. Atheism he defined as "the system which teaches that there is no God, and that it is impossible for man to know that there is a God." At least this is how Professor Flint is reported in the newspapers, although we hope he was not guilty of so idiotic a jumble.

Where are the Atheists who say there is no God? What are their names? Having mingled much with thoroughgoing sceptics, and read many volumes of heretical literature, we can confidently defy Professor Flint to produce the names of half a dozen dogmatic Atheists, and we will give him the whole world's literature to select from. Does he think that the brains of an Atheist are addled? If not, why does he make the Atheist first affirm that there is no God, and then affirm the impossibility of man's ever knowing whether there is a God or not? How could a man who holds his judgment in suspense, or who thinks the universal mystery insoluble to us, dogmatise upon the question of God's existence? If Professor Flint will carefully and candidly study sceptical literature, he will find that the dogmatic Atheist is as rare a the phoenix, and that those who consider the extant evidences of Theism inadequate, do not go on to affirm an universal negative, but content themselves with expressing their ignorance of Nature's why. For the most part they endorse Thomas Cooper's words, "I do not say there is no God, but this I say, I know not" Of course this modesty of affirmation may seem impiously immodest to one who has been trained and steeped in Theism so long that the infinite universe has become quite explicable to him; but to the sceptic it seems more wise and modest to confess one's ignorance, than to make false pretensions of knowledge.

Professor Flint "characterised the objections which Atheism urges against the existence of God as extremely feeble." Against the existence of what God? There be Gods many and Lords many; which of the long theological list is to be selected as the God? A God, like everything else from the heights to the depths, can be known only by his attributes; and what the Atheist does is not to argue against the existence of any God, which would be sheer lunacy, but to take the attributes affirmed by Theism as composing its Deity and inquire whether they are compatible with each other and with the facts of life. Finding that they are not, the Atheist simply sets Theism aside as not proven, and goes on his way without further afflicting himself with such abstruse questions.

The Atheist must be a very dreary creature, thinks Professor Flint. But why? Does he know any Atheists, and has he found them one half as dreary as Scotch Calvinists? It may seem hard to the immoderately selfish that some Infinite Spirit is not looking after their little interests, but it is assuredly a thousandfold harder to think that this Infinite Spirit has a yawning hell ready to engulph the vast majority of the world's miserable sinners. If the Atheist has no heaven, he has also no hell, which is a most merciful relief. Far better were universal annihilation than that even the meanest life should writhe for ever in hell, gnawed by the worm which never dieth, and burnt in the fire which is never quenched.

Even Nature, thinks Professor Flint, cannot be contemplated by the

Atheist as the Theist contemplates it; for while the latter views it as God's vesture wherewith he hides from us his intolerable glory, the latter views it as the mere embodiment of force, senseless, aimless, pitiless, an enormous mechanism grinding on of itself from age to age, but towards no God and for no good. Here we must observe that the lecturer trespasses beyond the truth. The Atheist does not affirm that Nature drives on to no God and no good; he simply says he knows not whither she is driving. And how many Theists are there who think of God in the presence of Nature, who see God's smile in the sunshine, or hear his wrath in the storm? Very few, we opine, in this practical sceptical age. To the Atheist as to the Theist, indeed to all blessed with vision, Nature is an ever new wonder of majesty and beauty! Sun, moon, and stars, earth, air, and sky, endure while the generations of men pass and perish; but every new generation is warmed, lighted, nurtured and gladdened by them with most sovereign and perfect impartiality. The loveliness and infinite majesty of Nature speak to all men, of all ages, climes and creeds. Not in her inanimate beauty do we find fatal objections to the doctrine of a wise and bountiful power which overrules her, but rather in the multiplied horrors, woes, and pangs of sentient life. When all actual and recorded misery is effaced, when no intolerable grief corrodes and no immedicable despair poisons life, when the tears of anguish are assuaged, when crime and vice are unknown and unremembered, and evil lusts are consumed in the fire of holiness; then, and then only, could we admit that a wise and righteous omnipotence rules the universal destinies. Until then we cannot recognise the fatherhood of God, but must find shelter and comfort in the more efficacious doctrine of the brotherhood of Man.

Professor Flint concluded his lecture, according to the newspaper report, thus:—"History bears witness that the declension of religion has ever been the decline of nations, because it has ever brought the decay of their moral life; and people have achieved noble things only when strongly animated by religious faith." All this is very poor stuff indeed to come from a learned professor. What nation has declined because of a relapse from religious belief? Surely not Assyria, Egypt, Greece, or Carthage? In the case of Rome, the decline of the empire was coincident with the rise of Christianity and the decline of Paganism; but the Roman Empire fell abroad mainly from political, and not from religious causes, as every student of history well knows. Christianity, that is the religion of the Bible, has been dying for nearly three centuries; and during that period, instead of witnessing a general degradation of mankind we have witnessed a marvellous elevation. The civilisation of to-day, compared with that which existed before Secular Science began her great battle with a tyrannous and obscurantist Church, is as a summer morn to a star-lit winter night.

Again, it is not true that men have achieved noble things only when strongly animated by religious faith; unless by "religious faith" be meant some vital idea or fervent enthusiasm. The three hundred Spartans who met certain death at Thermopylae died for a religious idea, but not for a theological idea, which is a very different thing. They perished to preserve the integrity of the state to which they belonged. The greatest Athenians were certainly not religious in Professor Flint's sense of the word, and the grand old Roman patriots had scarcely a scintillation of such a religious faith as he speaks of. Their religion was simply patriotism, but it was quite as operant and effective as Christian piety has ever been. Was it religious faith or patriotism which banded Frenchmen together in defiance of all Europe, and made them march to death as a bridegroom hastens to his bride? And in our own history have not our greatest achievers of noble things been very indifferent to theological dogmas? Nay, in all ages, have not the noblest laborers for human welfare been impelled by an urgent enthusiasm of humanity rather than by any supernatural faith? Professor Flint may rest assured that even though all "the old faiths ruin and rend," the human heart will still burn, and virtue and beauty still gladden the earth, although divorced from the creeds which held them in the thraldom of an enforced marriage.

A HIDDEN GOD

(October, 1879)

The Christian World is distinguished among religious journals by a certain breadth and vigor. On all social and political subjects it is remarkably advanced and outspoken, and its treatment of theological questions is far more liberal and intelligent than sceptics would expect. Of late years it has opened its columns to correspondence on many topics, some of a watery character, like the reality of Noah's flood, and others of a burning kind, like the doctrine of eternal punishment, on all of which great freedom of expression has been allowed. The editor himself, who is, we suspect, far more sceptical than most of his readers, has had his say on the question of Hell, and it is to be inferred from his somewhat guarded utterance that he has little belief in any such place. This, however, we state with considerable hesitation, for the majority of Christians still regard the doctrine of everlasting torture as indubitable and sacred, and we have no desire to lower him in the estimation of the Christian world in which he labors, or to cast a doubt on the orthodoxy of his creed. But the editor will not take it amiss if we insist that his paper is liberal in its Christianity, and unusually tolerant of unbelief.

Yet, while entitled to praise on his ground, the Christian World deserves something else than praise on another. It has recently published a series of articles for the purpose of stimulating faith and allaying doubt. If undertaken by a competent writer, able and willing to face the mighty difference between Christianity and the scientific spirit of our age, such a series of articles might be well worth reading. We might then admire if we could not agree, and derive benefit from friendly contact with an antagonist mind. But the writer selected for the task appears to possess neither of these qualifications. Instead of thinking he gushes; instead of reason he supplies us with unlimited sentiment. We expect to tread solid ground, or at least to find it not perilously soft; and lo! the soil is moist, and now and then we find ourselves up to the knees in unctuous mud. How difficult it is nowadays to discover a really argumentative Christian! The eminent favorites of orthodoxy write sentimental romances and call them "Lives of Christ," and preach sermons with no conceivable relation to the human intellect; while the apologists of faith imitate the tactics of the cuttle-fish, and when pursued cast out their opaque fluid of sentimentality to conceal their position. They mostly dabble in the shallows of scepticism, never daring to venture in the deeps; and what they take pride in as flashes of spiritual light resembles neither the royal gleaming of the sun nor the milder radiance of the moon, but rather the phosphorescence of corruption.

In the last article of the series referred to, entitled "Thou art a God that Hidest Thyself," there is an abundance of fictitious emotion and spurious rhetoric. From beginning to end there is a painful strain that never relaxes, reminding us of singers who pitch their voices too high and have to render all the upper notes in falsetto. An attempt is made to employ poetical imagery, but it ludicrously fails. The heaven of the Book of Revelation, with its gold and silver and precious stones, is nothing but a magnified jeweller's shop, and a study of it has influenced the style of later writers. At present Christian gushers have descended still lower, dealing not even in gold and jewels, but in Brummagem and paste. The word gem is greatly in vogue. Talmage uses it about twenty times in every lecture, Parker delights in it, and it often figures on the pages of serious books. In the article before us it is made to do frequent service. A promise of redemption is represented as shining gem-like on the brow of Revelation, Elims gem the dark bosom of the universal desert, and the morning gleams on the dew-gemmed earth. Perhaps a good recipe for this kind of composition would be an hour's gloat on the flaming window of a jeweller's shop in the West End.

But let us deal with the purport and purpose of the article. It aims at showing that God hides himself, and why he does so. The fact which it is attempted to explain none will deny. Moses ascended Mount Sinai to see God and converse with him, Abraham and God walked and talked together, and according to St. Paul the Almighty is not far from any one of us. But the modern mind is not prone to believe these things. The empire of reason has been enlarged at the expense of faith, whose provinces have one after another been annexed until only a small territory is left her, and that she finds it difficult to keep. Coincidently, God has become less and less a reality and more and more a dream. The reign of law is perceived everywhere, and all classes of phenomena may be explained without recourse to supernatural power. When Napoleon objected to Laplace that divine design was omitted from his mechanical theory of the universe, the French philosopher characteristically replied: "I had no need of that hypothesis." And the same disposition prevails in other departments of science. Darwin, for instance, undertakes to explain the origin and development of man, physical, intellectual and moral, without assuming any cause other than those which obtain wherever life exists. God is being slowly but surely driven from the domain of intermediate causes, and transformed into an ultimate cause, a mere figment of the imagination. He is being banished from nature into that poetical region inhabited by the gods of Polytheism, to keep company there with Jupiter and Apollo and Neptune and Juno and Venus, and all the rest of that glorious Pantheon. He no longer rules the actual life and struggle of the world, but lives at peace with his old rivals in—

> "The lucid interspace of world and world,
> Where never creeps a cloud or moves a wind,
> Nor ever falls the least white star of snow,
> Nor ever lowest roll of thunder moans;
> Nor sound of human sorrow mounts, to mar
> Their sacred everlasting calm." [1]

The essence of all this is admitted by the writer in the Christian World; he admits the facts, but denies the inference. They show us one of God's ways of hiding himself. Order prevails, but it is the expression of God's will, and not a mere result of the working of material forces. He operates by method, not by caprice, and hence the unchanging stability of things. While doing nothing in particular, he does everything in general. And this idea must be extended to human history. God endows man with powers, and allows him freedom to employ them as he will. But, strangely enough, God has a way of "ruling our freedom," and always there is "a restraining and restoring hand." How man's will can be free and yet overruled passes our merely carnal understanding, although it may be intelligible enough to minds steeped in the mysteries of theology. According to this writer, God's government of mankind is a "constitutional kingdom." Quite so. It was once arbitrary and despotic; now it is far milder and less exacting, having dwindled into the "constitutional" stage, wherein the King reigns but does not

---

[1] Tennyson: "Lucretius."

govern. Will the law of human growth and divine decay stop here? We think not. As the despotism has changed to a constitutional monarchy, so that will change to a republic, and the empty throne be preserved among other curious relics of the past.

God also hides himself in history. Although unapparent on the surface of events, his spirit is potent within them. "What," the writer asks, "is history—with all its dark passages of horror, its stormy revolutions, its ceaseless conflict, its tears, its groans, its blood—but the chronicle of an ever-widening realm of light, of order, of intelligence, wisdom, truth, and charity?" But if we admit the progress, we need not explain it as the work of God. Bunsen wrote a book on "God in History," which a profane wag said should have been called "Bunsen in History;" yet his attempt to justify the ways of God to men was not very successful. It is simply a mockery to ask us to believe that the slow progress of humanity must be attributed to omniscient omnipotence. A God who can evolve virtue and happiness only out of infinite evil and misery, and elevate us only through the agency of perpetual blood and tears, is scarcely a being to be loved and worshipped, unless we assume that his power and wisdom are exceedingly limited. Are we to suppose that God has woven himself a garment of violence, evil, and deceit, in order that we might not see too clearly his righteousness, goodness, and truth?

It must further be observed that Christian Theists cannot be permitted to ascribe all the good in the world to God, and all the evil to man, or else leave it absolutely unexplained. In the name of humanity we protest against this indignity to our race. Let God be responsible for good and evil both, or for neither; and if man is to consider himself chargeable with all the world's wrong, he should at least be allowed credit for all the compensating good.

The theory of evolution is being patronised by Theists rather too fulsomely. Not long ago they treated it with obloquy and contempt, but now they endeavor to use it as an argument for their faith, and in doing so they distort language as only theological controversialists can. Changing "survival of the fittest" into "survival of the best," they transform a physical fact into a moral law; and thus, as they think, take a new north-west passage to the old harbor of "whatever is is right." But while-evolution may be construed as progress, which some would contest, it cannot be construed as the invariable survival of the best; nor, if it were, could the process by which this result is achieved be justified. For evolution works through a universal struggle for existence, in which the life and well-being of some can be secured only through the suffering and final extinction of others; and even in its higher stages, cunning and unscrupulous strength frequently overcomes humane wisdom fettered by weakness. "Nature, red in tooth and claw, with ravin shrieks against the creed" of the Theist. If God is working through evolution, we must admit that he has marvellously hidden himself, and agree with the poet that he does "move in a mysterious way his wonders to perform."

The writer in the Christian World borrows an image from the puling scepticism of "In Memoriam," which describes man as

> *"An infant crying in the night,*
> *And with no language but a cry."*

This image of the infant is put to strange use. The writer says that God is necessarily hidden from us because we can grasp "his inscrutable nature and methods" only as "an infant can grasp the thought and purpose of a man." Similes are dangerous things. When it is demanded that they shall run upon all fours, they often turn against their masters. This one does so. The infant grows into a man in due course, and then he can not only grasp the thought and purpose of his father, but also, it may be, comprehend still greater things. Will the infant mind of man, when it reaches maturity, be thus related to God's? If not, the analogy is fallacious. Man is quite mature enough already, and has been so for thousands of years, to understand something of God's thought and purpose if he had only chosen to reveal them. This, however, if there be a God, he has not condescended to do. An appeal to the various pretended revelations of the world serves to convince us that all are the words of fallible men. Their very discord discredits them. As D'Holbach said, if God had spoken, the universe would surely be convinced, and the same conviction would fill every breast.

The reason given for God's hiding himself is very curious. "If," says the writer, "the way of God were not in large measure hidden, it would mean that we could survey all things from the height and the depth of God." Truly an awful contemplation! May it not be that God is hidden from us because there is none to be revealed, that "all the oracles are dumb or cheat because they have no secret to express"?

But, says the writer in the Christian World, there is one revelation of God that can never be gainsaid; "while the Cross stands as earth's most sacred symbol, there can be no utter hiding of his love." This, however, we venture to dispute. That Cross which was laid upon the back of Jesus poor mankind has been compelled to carry ever since, with no Simon to ease it of the load. Jesus was crucified on Calvary, and in his name man has suffered centuries of crucifixion. The immolation of Jesus can be no revelation of God's love. If the Nazarene was God, his crucifixion involves a complicated arrangement for murder; the Jews who demanded his death were divinely instigated, and Judas Iscariot was pre-ordained to betray his master; in which case his treachery was a necessary element of the drama, entitling him not to vituperation but to gratitude, even perhaps to the monument which Benjamin Disraeli suggested as his proper reward. Looking also at the history of Christianity, and seeing how the Cross has sheltered oppressors of mind and body, sanctioned immeasurable shedding of blood, and frightened peoples from freedom, while even now it symbolises all that is reactionary and accursed in Europe, we are constrained to say that the love it reveals is as noxious as the vilest hate.

GENERAL JOSHUA

(April, 1882)

Mountebank Talmage has just preached a funeral sermon on General Joshua. It is rather behind date, as the old warrior has been dead above three thousand years. But better late than never. Talmage tells us many things about Joshua which are not in the Bible, and some sceptics will say that his panegyric is a sheer invention. They may, however, be mistaken. The oracle of the Brooklyn Jabbernacle is known to be inspired. God holds converse with him, and he is thus enabled to supply us with fresh facts about Jehovah's fighting-cock from the lost books of Jasher and the Wars of the Lord.

Joshua, says Talmage, was a magnificent fighter. We say, he was a magnificent butcher. Jehovah did the fighting.

He was the virtual commander of the Jewish hosts; he won all their victories; and Joshua only did the slaughter. He excelled in that line of business. He delighted in the dying groans of women and children, and loved to dabble his feet and hands in the warm blood of the slain. No "Chamber of Horrors" contains the effigy of any wretch half so bloodthirsty and cruel.

According to Talmage, Joshua "always fought on the right side." Wars of conquest are never right. Thieving other people's lands is an abominable crime. The Jews had absolutely no claim to the territory they took possession of, and which they manured with the blood of its rightful owners. We know they said that God told them to requisition that fine little landed estate of Canaan. Half the thieves in history have said the same thing. We don't believe them. God never told any man to rob his neighbor, and whoever says so lies. The thief's statement does not suffice. Let him produce better evidence. A rascal who steals and murders cannot be believed on his oath, and 'tis more likely that he is a liar than that God is a scoundrel.

Talmage celebrates "five great victories" of Joshua. He omits two mighty achievements. General Joshua circumcised a million and a half Jews in a single day. His greatest battle never equalled that wonderful feat. The amputations were done at the rate of over a thousand a minute. Samson's jaw-bone was nothing to Joshua's knife. This surprising old Jew was as great in oratory as in surgery. On one occasion he addressed an audience of three millions, and everyone heard him. His voice must have reached two or three miles. No wonder the walls of Jericho fell down when Joshua joined in the shout. We dare say the Jews wore ear-preservers to guard their tympanums against the dreadful artillery of his speech.

Joshua's first victory, says Tahnage, was conquering the spring freshet of Jordan. As a matter of fact, Jehovah transacted that little affair. See, says Talmage, "one mile ahead go two priests carrying a glittering box four feet long and two feet wide. It is the Ark of the Covenant." He forgets to add that the Jew God was supposed to be inside it. Jack in the box is nothing to God in a box. What would have happened if the Ark had been buried with Jehovah safely fastened in? Would his godship have mouldered to dust? In that case he would never have seduced a carpenter's wife, and there would have been no God the Son as the fruit of his adultery.

Talmage credits General Joshua with the capture of Jericho. The Bible says that Jehovah overcame it. Seven priests went blowing rams' horns round the city for seven days. On the seventh day they went round it seven times. It must have been tiresome work, for Jericho was a large city several miles in circumference. But priests are always good "Walkers." After the last blowing of horns all the Jews shouted "Down Jericho, down Jericho!" This is Talmage's inspired account. The Bible states nothing of the kind. Just as the Islamites cry "Allah, Il Allah," it is probable that the Jews cried "Jahveh, Jahveh." But Talmage and the Bible both agree that when their shout rent the air the walls of Jericho fell flat—as flat as the fools who believe it.

Then, says Talmage, "the huzza of the victorious Israelites and the groan of the conquered Canaanites commingle!" Ah, that groan! Its sound still curses the Bible God. Men, women and children, were murdered. The very cattle, sheep and asses, were killed with the sword. Only one woman's house was spared, and she was a harlot.

It is as if the German army took Paris, and killed every inhabitant except Cora Pearl. This is inspired war, and Talmage glories in it. He would consider it an honor to be bottle-washer to such a pious hero as General Joshua. When Ai was taken, all its people were slaughtered, without any regard to age or sex. Talmage grins with delight, and cries "Bravo, Joshua!" The King of Ai was reserved for sport. They hung him on a tree and enjoyed the fun. Talmage approves this too. Everything Joshua did was right. Talmage is ready to stake his own poor little soul on that.

Joshua's victory over the five kings calls forth a burst of supernatural eloquence. Talmage pictures the "catapults of the sky pouring a volley of hailstones" on the flying Amorites, and words almost fail him to describe the glorious miracle of the lengthening of the day in order that Jehovah's prize-fighters might go on killing.

One passage is almost sublime. It is only one step off. "What," asks Talmage, "is the matter with Joshua? Has he fallen in an apoplectic fit? No. He is in prayer." Our profanity would not have gone to that length. But we take Talmage's word for it that prayer and apoplexy are very much alike.

The five kings were decapitated. "Ah," says Talmage, "I want five more kings beheaded to-day, King Alcohol, King Fraud, King Lust, King Superstition, and King Infidelity." Soft, you priestly calumniator! What right have you to associate Infidelity with fraud and lust? That Freethought, which you call "infidelity," is more faithful to truth and justice than your creed has ever been. And it will not be disposed of so easily as you think. You will never behead us, but we shall strangle you. We are crushing the life out of your wretched faith, and your spasmodic sermons are only the groans of its despair.

Talmage's boldest step on the line which separates the ludicrous from the sublime occurs in his peroration. He makes General Joshua conquer Death by lying down and giving up the ghost, and then asks for a headstone and a foot-stone for the holy corpse. "I imagine," he says, "that for the head it shall be the sun that stood still upon Gibeon, and for the foot the moon that stood still in the valley of Ajalon." This is about the finest piece of Yankee buncombe extant. If the sun and moon keep watch over General Joshua's grave, what are we to do? When we get to the New Jerusalem we shall want neither of these luminaries, for the glory of the Lord will shine upon us. But until then we cannot dispense with them, and we decidedly object to their being retained as perpetual mourners over Joshua's grave. If, however, one of them must do service, we humbly beg that it may be the moon. Let the sun illumine us by day, so that we may see to transact our affairs. And if ever we should long to behold "pale Dians beams" again, we might take Talmage as our guide to the unknown grave of General Joshua, and while they played softly over the miraculous two yards of turf we should see his fitting epitaph—Moonshine.

GOING TO HELL

(June, 1882)

Editing a Freethought paper is a dreadful business. It brings one into contact with many half-baked people who have little patent recipes for hastening the millennium; with ambitious versifiers who think it a disgrace to journalism that their productions are not instantly inserted; with discontented ladies and gentlemen who fancy that a heterodox paper is the proper vehicle for every species of complaint; and with a multitude of other bores too numerous to mention and too various to classify. But the worst of all are the anonymous bores, who send their insults, advice, or warnings, through the post for the benefit of the Queen's revenue. We generally pitch their puerile missives into the waste-paper basket; but occasionally we find one diverting enough to be introduced to our readers. A few days ago we received the following lugubrious epistle, ostensibly from a parson in Worcestershire, as the envelope bore the postmark of Tything.

"The fool hath said in his heart 'there is no God'—I have seen one of your blasphemous papers; and I say solemnly, as a clergyman of the Church of England, that I believe you are doing the work of the Devil, and are on the road to hell, and will spend eternity with the Devil, unless God, in his mercy, lead you, by the Holy Spirit, to repentance. Nothing is impossible, with him. A Dean in the Church of England says, 'Be wise, and laugh not through a speck of time, and then wail through an immeasurable eternity.' Except you change your views you will most certainly hear Christ say, at the Judgment Day, 'Depart ye cursed into everlasting fire prepared for the Devil and his angels.' (Matt, xxv.)"

This is a tolerably warm, though not very elegant effusion, and it is really a pity that so grave a counsellor should conceal his name; for if it should lead to our conversion, we should not know whom to thank for having turned us out of the primrose path to the everlasting bonfire. Our mentor assures us that with God nothing is impossible. We are sorry to learn this; for we must conclude that he does not take sufficient trouble with parsons to endow them with the courage of their convictions, or to make them observe the common decencies of epistolary intercourse.

This anonymous parson, who acts like an Irish "Moonlighter," and masks his identity while venting his spleen, presumes to anticipate the Day of Judgment, and tells exactly what Jesus Christ will say to us on that occasion. We are obliged to him for the information, but we wonder how he obtained it. The twenty-fifth of Matthew, to which he refers us, contains not a word about unbelievers. It simply states that certain persons, who have treated the Son of Man very shabbily in his distress, shall be sent to keep company with Old Nick and his imps. Now, we have never shown the Son of Man any incivility, much less any inhumanity, and we therefore repudiate this odious insinuation. Whenever Jesus Christ sends us a message that he is sick, we will pay him a visit; if he is hungry, we will find him a dinner; if he is thirsty, we will stand whatever he likes to drink; if he is naked, we will hunt him up a clean shirt and an old suit; and if he is in prison, we will, according as he is innocent or guilty, try to procure his release, or leave him to serve out his term. We should be much surprised if any parson in the three kingdoms would do any more Some of them, we believe, would see him condemned (new version) before they would lift a finger or spend sixpence to-help him.

We are charged with doing the work of the Devil. This is indeed news. We never knew the Devil required any assistance. He was always very active and enterprising, and quite able to manage his own business. And although his rival, Jehovah, is so dotingly senile as to yield up everything to his mistress and her son, no one has ever whispered the least hint of the Devil's decline into the same abject position. But if his Satanic Majesty needed our aid we should not be loth to give it, for after carefully reading the Bible many times from beginning to end, we have come to the conclusion that he is about the only gentleman in it.

We are "on the road to hell." Well, if we must go somewhere, that is just the place we should choose. The temperature is high, and it would no doubt at first be incommodious. But, as old Sir Thomas Browne says, afflictions induce callosities, and in time we should get used to anything.

When once we grew accustomed to the heat, how thankful we should be at having escaped the dreary insipidity of heaven, with its perpetual psalms, its dolorous trumpets, its gruesome elders, and its elderly beasts! How thankful at having missed an eternity with Abraham, Isaac, Jacob, David, and all the many blackguards and scoundrels of the Bible! How thankful at having joined for ever the society of Rabelais, Bruno, Spinoza, Voltaire, Thomas Paine, John Stuart Mill, and all the great poets, sages and wits, who possess so much of that carnal wisdom which is at enmity with the pious folly of babes and sucklings!

On the whole, we think it best to keep on our present course. Let the bigots rave and the parsons wail. They are deeply interested in the doctrine of heaven and hell beyond the grave. We believe in heaven and hell on this side of it; a hell of ignorance, crime, and misery; a heaven of wisdom, virtue, and happiness. Our duty is to promote the one and combat the other. If there be a just God, the fulfilment of that duty will suffice; if God be unjust, all honest men will be in the same boat, and have the courage to despise and defy him.

CHRISTMAS EVE IN HEAVEN

(December, 1881)

Christmas Eve had come and almost gone. It was drawing nigh midnight, and I sat solitary in my room, immersed in memory, dreaming of old days and their buried secrets. The fire, before which I mused, was burning clear without flame, and its intense glow, which alone lighted my apartment, cast a red tint on the furniture and walls. Outside the streets were muffled deep with snow, in which no footstep was audible. All was quiet as death, silent as the grave, save for the faint murmur of my own breathing. Time and space seemed annihilated beyond those four narrow walls, and I was as a coffined living centre of an else lifeless infinity.

My reverie was rudely broken by the staggering step of a fellow-lodger, whose devotion to Bacchus was the one symptom of reverence in his nature. He reeled up stair after stair, and as he passed my door he lurched against it so violently that I feared he would come through. But he slowly recovered himself after some profane mutterings, reeled up the next flight of stairs, and finally deposited his well-soaked clay on the bed in his own room immediately over mine.

After this interruption my thoughts changed most fancifully. Why I know not, but I began to brood on the strange statement of Saint Paul concerning the man who was lifted up into the seventh heaven, and there beheld things not lawful to reveal. While pondering this story I was presently aware of an astonishing change. The walls of my room slowly expanded, growing ever thinner and thinner, until they became the filmiest transparent veil which at last dissolved utterly away. Then (whether in the spirit or the flesh I know not) I was hurried along through space, past galaxy after galaxy of suns and stars, separate systems yet all mysteriously related.

Swifter than light we travelled, I and my unseen guide, through the infinite ocean of ether, until our flight was arrested by a denser medium, which I recognised as an atmosphere like that of our earth. I had scarcely recovered from this new surprise when (marvel of marvels!) I found myself before a huge gate of wondrous art and dazzling splendor. At a word from my still unseen guide it swung open, and I was urged within. Beneath my feet was a solid pavement of gold. Gorgeous mansions, interspersed with palaces, rose around me, and above them all towered the airy pinnacles of a matchless temple, whose points quivered in the rich light like tongues of golden fire. The walls glittered with countless rubies, diamonds, pearls, amethysts, emeralds, and other precious stones; and lovely presences, arrayed in shining garments, moved noiselessly from place to place. "Where am I?" I ejaculated, half faint with wonder. And my hitherto unseen guide, who now revealed himself, softly answered, "In Heaven."

Thereupon my whole frame was agitated with inward laughter. I in Heaven, whose fiery doom had been prophesied so often by the saints on earth! I, the sceptic, the blasphemer, the scoffer at all things sacred, who had laughed at the legends and dogmas of Christianism as though they were incredible and effete as the myths of Olympus! And I thought to myself, "Better I had gone straight to Hell, for here in the New Jerusalem they will no doubt punish me worse than there." But my angelic guide, who read my thought, smiled benignly and said, "Fear not, no harm shall happen to you. I have exacted a promise of safety for you, and here no promise can be broken." "But why," I asked, "have you brought me hither, and how did you obtain my guarantee of safety?" And my guide answered, "It is our privilege each year to demand one favor which may not be refused; I requested that I might bring you here; but I did not mention your name, and if you do nothing outrageous you will not be noticed, for no one here meddles with another's business, and our rulers are too much occupied with foreign affairs to trouble about our domestic concerns." "Yet," I rejoined, "I shall surely be detected, for I wear no heavenly robe." Then my guide produced one from a little packet, and having donned it, I felt safe from the fate of him who was expelled because he had not on a wedding-garment at the marriage feast.

As we moved along, I inquired of my guide why he took such interest in me; and he replied, looking sadly, "I was a sceptic on earth centuries ago, but I stood alone, and at last on my death-bed, weakened by sickness, I again embraced the creed of my youth and died in the Christian faith. Hence my presence in Heaven. But gladly would I renounce Paradise even for Hell, for those figures so lovely without are not all lovely within, and I would rather consort with the choicer spirits who abide with Satan and hold high revel of heart and head in his court. Yet wishes are fruitless; as the tree falls it lies, and my lot is cast for ever." Whereupon I laid my hand in his, being speechless with grief!

We soon approached the magnificent temple, and entering it we mixed with the mighty crowd of angels who were witnessing the rites of worship performed by the elders and beasts before the great white throne. All happened exactly as Saint John describes. The angels rent the air with their acclamations, after the inner circle had concluded, and then the throne was deserted by its occupants.

My dear guide then led me through some narrow passages until we emerged into a spacious hall, at one end of which hung a curtain. Advancing towards this with silent tread, we were able to look through a slight aperture, where the curtain fell away from the pillar, into the room beyond. It was small and cosy, and a fire burned in the grate, before which sat poor dear God the Father in a big arm-chair. Divested of his godly paraphernalia, he looked old and thin, though an evil fire still gleamed from his cavernous eyes. On a table beside him stood some phials, one of which had seemingly just been used. God the Son stood near, looking much younger and fresher, but time was beginning to tell on him also. The Ghost flitted about in the form of a dove, now perching on the Father's shoulder and now on the head of the Son.

Presently the massive bony frame of the Father was convulsed with a fit of coughing; Jesus promptly applied a restorative from the phial, and after a terrible struggle the cough was subdued. During this scene the Dove fluttered violently from wall to wall. When the patient was thoroughly restored the following conversation ensued:—

Jesus.—Are you well now, my Father?

Jehovah.—Yes, yes, well enough. Alack, how my strength wanes! Where is the pith that filled these arms when I fought for my chosen people? Where the fiery vigor that filled my veins when I courted your mother?

(Here the Dove fluttered and looked queer.)

Jesus.—Ah, sire, do not speak thus. You will regain your old strength.

Jehovah.—Nay, nay, and you know it. You do not even wish me to recover, for in my weakness you exercise sovereign power and rule as you please.

Jesus.—O sire, sire!

Jehovah.—Come now, none of these demure looks. We know each other too well. Practise before the saints if you like, but don't waste your acting on me.

Jesus.—My dear Father, pray curb your temper. That is the very thing the people on earth so much complain of.

Jehovah.—My dearly beloved Son, in whom I am not at all well pleased, desist from this hypocrisy. Your temper is as bad as mine. You've shed blood enough in your time, and need not rail at me.

Jesus.—Ah, sire, only the blood of heretics.

Jehovah.—Heretics, forsooth! They were very worthy people for the most part, and their only crime was that they neglected you. But why should we wrangle? We stand or fall together, and I am falling. Satan draws most souls from earth to his place, including all the best workers and thinkers, who are needed to sustain our drooping power; and we receive nothing but the refuse; weak, slavish, flabby souls, hardly worth saving or damning; gushing preachers, pious editors, crazy enthusiasts, and half-baked old ladies of both sexes. Why didn't you preach a different Gospel while you were about it? You had the chance once and let it slip: we shall never have another.

Jesus.—My dear Father, I am reforming my Gospel to make it suit the altered taste of the times.

Jehovah.—Stuff and nonsense! It can't be done; thinking people see through it; the divine is immutable. The only remedy is to start afresh. Could I beget a new son all might be rectified; but I cannot, I am too old. Our dominion is melting away like that of all our predecessors. You cannot outlast me, for I am the fountain of your life; and all the multitude of "immortal" angels who throng our court, live only while I uphold them, and with me they will vanish into eternal limbo.

Here followed another fit of coughing worse than before. Jesus resorted again to the phial, but the cordial seemed powerless against this sharp attack. Just then the Dove fluttered against the curtain, and my guide hurried me swiftly away.

In a corridor of the temple we met Michael and Raphael. The latter scrutinised me so closely that my blood ran cold; but just when my dread was deepest his countenance cleared, and he turned towards his companion. Walking behind the great archangels we were able to hear their conversation. Raphael had just returned from a visit to the earth, and he was reporting to Michael a most alarming defection from the Christian faith. People, he said, were leaving in shoals, and unless fresh miracles were worked he trembled for the prospects of the dynasty. But what most alarmed him was the spread of profanity. While in England he had seen copies of a blasphemous paper which horrified the elect by ridiculing the Bible in what a bishop had justly called "a heartless and cruel way." "But, my dear Michael," continued Raphael, "that is not all, nor even the worst. This scurrilous paper, which would be quickly suppressed if we retained our old influence, actually caricatures our supreme Lord and his heavenly host in woodcuts, and thousands of people enjoy this wicked profanity. I dare say our turn will soon come, and we shall be held up to ridicule like the rest." "Impossible!" cried Michael; "Surely there is some mistake. What is the name of this abominable print?" With a grave look, Raphael replied: "No, Michael, there is no mistake. The name of this imp of blasphemy is—I hesitate to say it—the Free—————"[2]

But at this moment my guide again hurried me along. We reached the splendid gate once more, which slowly opened and let us through. Again we flew through the billowy ether, sweeping past system after system with intoxicating speed, until at last, dazed and almost unconscious, I regained this earthly shore. Then I sank into a stupor. When I awoke the fire had burnt down to the last cinder, all was dark and cold, and I shivered as I tried to stretch my half-cramped limbs. Was it all a dream? Who can say? Whether in the spirit or the flesh I know not, said Saint Paul, and I am compelled to echo his words. Sceptics may shrug their shoulders, smile, or laugh; but "there are more things in heaven and earth than are dreamt of in their philosophy."

---

[2] Was it the Freethinker?

PROFESSOR BLACKIE ON ATHEISM

(January, 1879)

Professor Blackie is a man with whom we cannot be angry, however greatly his utterances are calculated to arouse that feeling. He is so impulsive, frank, and essentially good-natured, that even his most provoking words call forth rather a smile of compassion than a frown of resentment. Those who know his character and position will yield him the widest allowance. His fiery nature prompts him to energetic speech on all occasions. But when his temper has been fretted, as it frequently is, by the boisterous whims of his Greek students in that most boisterous of universities, it is not surprising if his expressions become splenetic even to rashness. The ingenuous Professor is quite impartial in his denunciations. He strikes out right and left against various objects of his dislike. Everything he dissents from receives one and the same kind of treatment, so that no opinion he assails has any special reason to complain; and every blow he deals is accompanied with such a jolly smile, sometimes verging into a hearty laugh, that no opponent can well refuse to shake hands with him when all is over.

This temper, however, is somewhat inconsistent with the scientific purpose indicated in the title of Professor Blackie's book. A zoologist who had such a particular and unconquerable aversion to one species of animals that the bare mention of its name made his gorge rise, would naturally give us a very inadequate and unsatisfactory account of it. So, in this case, instead of getting a true natural history of Atheism, which would be of immense service to every thinker, we get only an emphatic statement of the authors' hatred of it under different aspects. Atheism is styled "a hollow absurdity," "that culmination of all speculative absurdities," "a disease of the speculative faculty," "a monstrous disease of the reasoning faculty," and so on.

The chapter on "Its Specific Varieties and General Root" is significantly headed with that hackneyed declaration of the Psalmist, "The fool hath said in his heart, There is no God," as though impertinence were better from a Jew than from a Christian, or more respectable for being three thousand years old. Perhaps Professor Blackie has never heard of the sceptical critic who exonerated the Psalmist on the ground that he was speaking jocosely, and really meant that the man who said in his heart only "There is no God," without saying so openly, was the fool. But this interpretation is as profane as the other is impertinent; and in fact does a great injustice to the Atheist, who has never been accustomed to say "There is no God," an assertion which involves the arrogance of infinite knowledge, since nothing less than that is requisite to prove an universal negative: but simply "I know not of such an existence," which is a modest statement intellectually and morally, and quite unlike the presumption of certain theologians who, as Mr. Arnold says, speak familiarly of God as though he were a man living in the next street.

For his own sake Professor Blackie should a little curb his proneness to the use of uncomplimentary epithets. He does himself injustice when he condescends to describe David Hume's theory of causation as "wretched cavil." Carlyle is more just to this great representative of an antagonistic school of thought. He exempts him from the sweeping condemnation of his contemporaries in Scottish prose literature, and admits that he was "too rich a man to borrow" from France or elsewhere. And surely Hume was no less honest than rich in thought. Jest and captiousness were entirely foreign to his mind. Wincing under his inexorable logic, the ontologist may try to console himself with the thought that the great sceptic was playing with arguments like a mere dialectician of wondrous skill; but in reality Hume was quite in earnest, and always meant what he said. We may also observe that it is Professor Blackie and not Darwin who suffers from the asking of such questions as these:—"What monkey ever wrote an epic poem, or composed a tragedy or a comedy, or even a sonnet? What monkey professed his belief in any thirty-nine articles, or well-compacted Calvinistic confession, or gave in his adhesion to any Church, established or disestablished?" If Mr. Darwin heard these questions he might answer with a good humored smile, "My dear sir, you quite mistake my theories, and your questions travesty them. I would further observe that while the composition of poems would unquestionably be creditable to monkeys, I, who have some regard for them as relatives, however distant, am heartily glad they have never done any of the other things you mention, which I deem a negative proof that their reason, though limited, is fortunately sane."

Professor Blackie's opening chapter on "Presumptions" fully justifies its title. The general consent of mankind in favor of Theism is assumed to have established its validity, and to have put Atheists altogether out of court; and a long list of illustrious Theists, from Solomon to Hegel, is contrasted with a meagre catalogue of Atheists, comprising only the names of David Hume, Jeremy Bentham, and John Stuart Mill.[3] Confucius and Buddha are classed

---

[3] Professor Blackie is singularly silent as to James Mill,
  the father of the celebrated Utilitarian philosopher, far
  more robust in intellect and character than his son. He is

apart, as lying "outside of our Western European Culture altogether," but with a promise that "in so far as they seem to have taught a morality without religion, or a religion without God, we shall say a word or two about them by-and-by." So far as Buddha is concerned this promise is kept; but in relation to Confucius it is broken. Probably the Chinese sage was found too tough and embarrassing a subject, and so it was thought expedient to ignore him for the more tractable prophet of India, whose doctrine of Transmigration might with a little sophistry be made to resemble the Christian doctrine of Immortality, and his Nirvana the Kingdom of Heaven.

What does the general consent of mankind prove in regard to beliefs like Theism? Simply nothing. Professor Blackie himself sees that on some subjects it is worthless, particularly when special knowledge or special faculty is required. But there are questions, he contends, which public opinion rightly decides, even though opposed to the conclusions of subtle thinkers. "Perhaps," he says, "we shall hit the mark here if we say broadly that, as nature is always right, the general and normal sentiment of the majority must always be right, in so far as it is rooted in the universal and abiding instincts of humanity; and public opinion, as the opinion of the majority, will be right also in all matters which belong to the general conduct of life among all classes, and with respect to which the mind of the majority has been allowed a perfectly free, natural, and healthy exercise." Now, in the first place, we must reiterate our opinion that the general consent of mankind on a subject like Theism proves absolutely nothing. It is perfectly valid on questions

---

the dominant figure of Mill's "Autobiography," and has about him a more august air than his son ever wore.

of ordinary taste and feeling, but loses all logical efficacy in relation to questions which cannot be determined by a direct appeal to experience. And undeniably Theism is one of those questions, unless we admit with the transcendentalist what is contrary to evident fact, that men have an intuitive perception of God. In the next place, the minor premise of this argument is assumed. There is no general consent of mankind in favor of Theism, but only a very extensive consent. Mr. Gladstone, not long since, in the Nineteenth Century, went so far as to claim the general consent of mankind in favor of Christianity, by simply excluding all heathen nations from a right to be heard. Professor Blackie does not go to this length, but his logical process is no different. Lastly, our author's concluding proviso vitiates his whole case; for if there be one question on which "the mind of the majority" has not been allowed a "perfectly free, natural, and healthy exercise," it is that of the existence of God. We are all prepossessed hi its favor by early training, custom, and authority. Our minds have never been permitted to play freely upon it. A century ago Atheists stood in danger of death; only recently have penal and invidious statutes against them been cancelled or mitigated; and even now bigotry against honest disbelief in Theism is so strong that a man often incurs greater odium in publicly avowing it than in constantly violating all the decalogue save the commandment against murder. Murderers and thieves, though punished here, are either forgotten or compassionated after death; but not even the grave effectually shields the Atheist from the malignity of pious zeal. Fortunately, however, a wise and humane tolerance is growing in the world, and extending towards the most flagrant heresies. Perhaps we shall ultimately admit with sage old Felltham, that "we fill the world with cruel brawls in the obstinate defence of that whereof we might with more honor confess ourselves to be ignorant," and that "it is no shame for man not to know that which is not in his possibility."

The causes of Atheism are, according to Professor Blackie, very numerous. He finds seven or eight distinct ones. The lowest class of Atheists are "Atheists of imbecility," persons of stunted intellect, incapable of comprehending the idea of God. These, however, he will not waste his time with, nor will we. He then passes to the second class of reprobates, whose Atheism springs not from defect of intellect, but from moral disorder, and who delight to conceive the universe as resembling their own chaos. These we shall dismiss, with a passing remark that if moral disorder naturally induces Atheism, some very eminent Christians have been marvellous hypocrites. Lack of reverence is the next cause of Atheism, and is indeed its "natural soil." But as Professor Blackie thinks this may be "congenital, like a lack of taste for music, or an incapacity of understanding a mathematical problem," we are obliged to consider this third class of Atheists as hopeless as the first. Having admitted that their malady may be congenital, our author inflicts upon these unfortunates a great deal of superfluous abuse, apparently forgetting that they are less to blame than their omnipotent maker. The fourth cause of Atheism is pride or self-will. But this seems very erratic in its operations, since the only two instances cited—namely, Napoleon the Great and Napoleon the Little, were certainly Theists. Next comes democracy, between which and irreverence there is a natural connexion, and from which, "as from a hotbed, Atheism in its rankest stage naturally shoots up." Professor Blackie, as may be surmised, tilts madly against this horrible foe. But it will not thus be subdued. Democracy is here and daily extending itself, overwhelming slowly but surely all impediments to its supremacy. If Theism is incompatible with it, then the days of Theism are numbered. Professor Blackie's peculiar Natural History of atheism is more likely to please the opposite ranks than his own, who may naturally cry out, with a sense of being sold, "call you that backing of your friends?"

Pride of intellect is the next cause of Atheism. Don Juan sells himself to perdition for a liberal share of pleasure, but Faust hankers only after forbidden knowledge. This is of various kinds; but "of all kinds, that which has long had the most evil reputation of begetting Atheism is Physical Science." Again does the fervid Professor set lance in rest, and dash against this new foe to Theism, much as Don Quixote charged the famous windmill. But science, like the windmill, is too big and strong to suffer from such assaults. The "father of this sort of nonsense," in modern times was David Hume, who, we are elegantly informed, was "a very clever fellow, a very agreeable, gentlemanly fellow too." His "nonsense about causation" is to be traced to a want of reverence in his character. Indeed, it seems that all persons who adhere to a philosophy alien to Professor Blackie's have something radically wrong with them. Let this Edinburgh Professor rail as he may, David Hume's theory of causation will suffer no harm, and his contrast of human architecture, which is mechanism, with natural architecture, which is growth, will still form an insuperable obstacle to that "natural theology" which, as Garth Wilkinson says with grim humor, seeks to elicit, or rather "construct," "a scientific abstraction answering to the concrete figure of the Vulcan of the Greeks—that is to say a universal Smith"!

Eventually Professor Blackie gets so sick of philosophers, that he turns from them to poets, who may more safely be trusted "in matters of healthy human sentiment." But here fresh difficulties arise. Although "a poet is naturally a religious animal," we find that the greatest of Roman poets Lucretius, was an Atheist, while even "some of our most brilliant notorieties in the modern world of song are not the most notable for piety." But our versatile Professor easily accounts for this by assuming that there "may be an idolatry of the imaginative, as well as of the knowing faculty." Never did natural historian so jauntily provide for every fact contravening his theories. Professor Blackie will never understand Atheism, or write profitably upon it, while he pursues this course. Let him restrain his discursive propensities, and deal scientifically with this one fact, which explodes his whole theory of Atheism. The supreme glory of our modern poetry is Shelley, and if ever a man combined splendor of imagination with keen intelligence and saintly character it was he. Raphael incarnate he seems, yet he stands outside all the creeds, and to his prophetic vision, in the sunlight of the world's great age begun anew, the—

> *Faiths and empires gleam*
> *Like wrecks of a dissolving dream.*

In his treatment of Buddhism Professor Blackie is candid and impartial, until he comes to consider its Atheistic character. Then his reason seems almost entirely to forsake him. After saying that "what Buddha preached was a gospel of pure human ethics, divorced not only from Brahma and the Brahminic Trinity, but even from the existence of God;" and describing Buddha himself as "a rare, exceptional, and altogether transcendental incarnation of moral perfection;" he first tries to show that Nirvana is the same as the Christian eternal life, and transmigration of souls a faithful counterpart of the Christian doctrine of future reward and punishment. Feeling, perhaps, how miserably he has failed in this attempt, he turns with exasperation on Buddhism, and affirms that it "can in no wise be looked upon as anything but an abnormal manifestation of the religious life of man." We believe that Professor Blackie himself must have already perceived the futility and absurdity of this.

The last chapter of Professor Blackie's book is entitled "The Atheism of Reaction." In it he strikes characteristically at the five points of Calvinism, at Original Guilt, Eternal Punishment, Creation out of Nothing, and Special Providence; which he charges with largely contributing to the spread of Atheism. While welcoming these assaults on superstition, we are constrained to observe that the Christian dogmas which Professor Blackie impugns and denounces are not specific causes of Atheism. Again he is on the wrong scent. The revolt against Theism at the present time is indeed mainly moral, but the preparation for it has been an intellectual one. Modern Science has demonstrated, for all practical purposes, the inexorable reign of law. The God of miracles, answering prayer and intimately related to his children of men, is an idea exploded and henceforth impossible. The only idea of God at all possible, is that of a supreme universal intelligence, governing nature by fixed laws, and apparently quite heedless whether their operation brings us joy or pain. This idea is intellectually permissible, but it is beyond all proof, and can be entertained only as a speculation. Now, the development of knowledge which makes this the only permissible idea of God, also changes Immortality from a religious certitude to an unverifiable supposition. The rectification of the evils of this life cannot, therefore, be reasonably expected in another; so that man stands alone, fighting a terrible battle, with no aid save from his own strength and skill. To believe that Omnipotence is the passive spectator of this fearful strife, is for many minds altogether too hard. They prefer to believe that the woes and pangs of sentient life were not designed; that madness, anguish, and despair, result from the interplay of unconscious forces. They thus set Theism aside, and unable to recognise the fatherhood of God, they cling more closely to the brotherhood of Man.

SALVATIONISM

(April, 1882)

There is no new thing under the sun, said the wise king Many a surprising novelty is only an old thing in a new dress. And this is especially true in respect to religion. Ever since the feast of Pentecost, when the Apostles all jabbered like madmen, Christianity has been marked by periodical fits of insanity. It would occupy too much space to enumerate these outbursts, which have occurred in every part of Christendom, but we may mention a few that have happened in our own country. During the Commonwealth, some of the numerous sects went to the most ludicrous extremes; preaching rousing sermons, praying through the nose, assuming Biblical names, and prophesying the immediate reign of the saints. There was a reaction against the excesses of Puritanism after the death of Cromwell; and until the time of Whitfield and Wesley religion continued to be a sober and respectable influence, chiefly useful to the sovereign and the magistrate. But these two powerful preachers rekindled the fire of religious enthusiasm in the hearts of the common people, and Methodism was founded among those whom the Church had scarcely touched. Not many years ago the Hallelujah Band spread itself far and wide, and then went out like a straw fire. And now we have Salvationism, doing just the same kind of work, and employing just the same kind of means. Will this new movement die away like so many others? It is difficult to say. Salvationism may be only a flash in the pan; but, on the other hand, it may provide the only sort of Christianity possible in an age of science and freethought. The educated classes and the intelligent artisans will more and more desert the Christian creed, and there will probably be left nothing but the dregs and the scum, for whom Salvationism is exactly suited. Christianity began among the poor, ignorant, and depraved; and it may possibly end its existence among the very same classes.

In all these movements we see a striking illustration of what the biologists call the law of Atavism. There is a constant tendency to return to the primitive type. We can form some idea of what early Christianity was by reading the Acts of the Apostles. The true believers went about preaching in season and out of season; they cried and prayed with a loud voice; they caused tumult in the streets, and gave plenty of trouble to the civil authorities. All this is true of Salvationism to-day; and we have no doubt that the early Church, under the guidance of Peter, was just a counterpart of the Salvation Army under "General" Booth—to the Jews, or men of the world, a stumbling-block, and to the Greeks, or educated thinkers, a folly.

Early Christians were "full of the Holy Ghost," that is of wild enthusiasm. Scoffers said they were drunk, and they acted like madmen. Leap across seventeen centuries, and we shall find Methodists acting in the same way. Wesley states in his Journal (1739) of his hearers at Wapping, that "some were torn with a kind of convulsive motion in every part of their bodies, and that so violently that often four or five persons could not hold one of them." And Lecky tells us, in his "History of the Eighteenth Century," that "religious madness, which from the nature of its hallucinations, is usually the most miserable of all the forms of insanity, was in this, as in many later revivals, of no unfrequent occurrence." Now Salvationism produces the very same effects. It drives many people mad; and it is a common thing for men and women at its meetings to shout, dance, jump, and finally fall on the floor in a pious ecstacy. While they are in this condition, the Holy

Ghost is entering them and the Devil is being driven out. Poor creatures! They take us back in thought to the days of demoniacal possession, and the strange old world that saw the devil-plagued swine of Gadara drowned in the sea.

The free and easy mingling of the sexes at these pious assemblies, is another noticeable feature. Love-feasts were a flagrant scandal in the early Church, and women who returned from them virtuous must have been miracles of chastity. Methodism was not quite so bad, but it tolerated some very strange pranks. The Rev. Richard Polwhele, in his "Anecdotes of Methodism" (a very rare book), says that "At St. Agnes, the Society stay up the whole night, when girls of twelve and fourteen years of age, run about the streets, calling out that they are possessed." He goes on to relate that at Probus "the preacher at a late hour of the night, after all but the higher classes left the room, would order the candles to be put out, and the saints fall down and kneel on their naked knees; when he would go round and thrust his hand under every knee to feel if it were bare." Salvationism does not at present go to this length, but it has still time enough to imitate all the freaks of its predecessor. There was an All-Night meeting in Whitechapel a few months ago, which threatened to develope into a thoroughgoing love-feast. The light was rather dim, voices grew low, cheeks came perilously near, and hands met caressingly. Of course it was nothing but the love of God that moved them, yet it looked like something else; and the uninitiated spectator of "the mystery of godliness" found it easy to understand how American camp-meetings tend to increase the population, and why a Magistrate in the South-west of England observed that one result of revivals in his district was a number of fatherless weans.

In one respect Salvationism excels all previous revivals. It is unparalleled in its vulgarity. The imbecile coarseness of its language makes one ashamed of human nature. Had it existed in Swift's time, he might have added a fresh clause to his terrible indictment of mankind. Its metaphors are borrowed from the slaughter-house, its songs are frequently coarser than those of the lowest music-hall, and the general style of its preaching is worthy of a congregation of drunken pugilists. The very names assumed by its officers are enough to turn one's stomach. Christianity has fallen low indeed when its champions boast such titles as the "Hallelujah Fishmonger," the "Blood-washed Miner," the "Devil Dodger," the "Devil Walloper," and "Gipsy Sal."

The constitution of the Salvation Army is a pure despotism. General Booth commands it absolutely. There is a Council of War, consisting of his own family. All the funds flow into his exchequer, and he spends them as he likes. No questions are allowed, no accounts are rendered, and everything is under his unqualified control. The "General" may be a perfectly honest man, but we are quite sure that none but pious lunatics would trust him with such irresponsible power.

We understand that the officials are all paid, and some of them extremely well. They lead a very pleasant life, full of agreeable excitement; they wear uniform, and are dubbed captain, major, or some other title. Add to all this, that they suppose themselves (when honest) to be particular favorites of God; and it will be easy to understand how so many of them prefer a career of singing and praying to earning an honest living by hard work, The Hallelujah lads and lasses could not, for the most part, get decent wages in any other occupation. All they require for this work is a good stomach and good lungs; and if they can only boast of having been the greatest drunkard in the district, the worst thief, or the most brutal character, they are on the high road to fortune, and may count on living in clover for the rest of their sojourn in this vale of tears.

A PIOUS SHOWMAN

(October, 1882)

We all remember how that clever showman, Barnum, managed to fan the Jumbo fever. When the enterprising Yankee writes his true autobiography we shall doubtless find some extraordinary revelations. Yet Barnum, after all, makes no pretence of morality or religion. He merely goes in for making a handsome fortune out of the curiosity and credulity of the public. If he were questioned as to his principles, he would probably reply like Artemus Ward—"Princerpuls? I've nare a one. I'm in the show bizniz."

General Booth is quite as much a showman as Barnum, but he is a pious showman. He is a perfect master of the vulgar art of attracting fools. Every day brings a fresh change in his "Walk up, Walk up." Tambourine girls, hallelujah lasses, converted clowns and fiddlers, sham Italian organ grinders, bands in which every man plays his own tune, officers in uniform, Davidic dances, and music-hall tunes, are all served up with a plentiful supply of blood and fire. The "General" evidently means to stick at nothing that will draw; and we quite believe that if a pair of Ezekiel's cherubim were available, he would worry God Almighty into sending them down for exhibition at the City Road show.

Booth's latest dodge is to say the least peculiar. Most fathers would shrink from trafficking in a son's marriage, but Booth is above such nice scruples. The worst deeds are sanctified by love of God, and religion condones every indecency.

Mr. Bramwell Booth, whom the General has singled out as his

apostolic successor, and heir to all the Army's property, got married last week; and the pious showman actually exhibited the bridegroom and bride to the public at a shilling a head. About three hundred pounds were taken at the doors, and a big collection was made inside. Booth's anxiety for the cash was very strongly illustrated. Commissioner Bailton, who has had a very eccentric career, was enjoying his long deferred opportunity of making a speech, when many of the crowd began to press towards the door. "Stop," cried Booth, "don't go yet, there's going to be a collection." But the audience melted faster than ever. Whereupon Booth jumped up again, stopped poor Railton unceremoniously, and shouted "Hold on, we'll make the collection now." This little manouvre was quite in keeping with the showman's instruction to his subalterns, to have plenty of good strong collecting boxes and pass them round often.

Booth's facetious remarks during his son's marriage according to the Army forms were well adapted to tickle the ears of his groundlings. The whole thing was a roaring farce, and well sustained the reputation of the show. There was also the usual spice of blasphemy. Before Bramwell Booth marched on to the platform a board was held up bearing the inscription "Behold the bridegroom cometh." These mountebanks have no reverence even for what they call sacred. They make everything dance to their tune. They prostitute "God's Word," caricature Jesus Christ, and burlesque all the watchwords and symbols of their creed.

One of Booth's remarks after the splicing was finished is full of suggestion. He said that his enemies might cavil, but he had found out a road to fortune in this world and the next. Well, the Lord only knows how he will fare in the next world, but in this world the pious showman has certainly gained a big success. He can neither write nor preach, and as for singing, a half a dozen notes from his brazen throat would empty the place as easily as a cry of "Fire." But he is a dexterous manager; he knows how to work the oracle; he understands catering for the mob; in short, he is a very clever showman, who deals in religion just as other showmen deal in wild animals, giants, dwarfs, two-headed sheep, fat women, and Siamese twins.

Fortune has brought to our hands a copy of a private circular issued by "Commissioner" Railton, soliciting wedding presents for Mr. Bramwell Booth. With the exception of Reuben May's begging letters, it is the finest cadging document we ever saw. Booth was evidently ashamed to sign it himself, so it bears the name of Railton. But the pious showman cannot disown the responsibility for it. He will not allow the officers of the Army to marry without his sanction; he forbids them to accept any private present; he keeps a sharp eye on every detail of the organisation. Surely, then, he will not have the face to say that he knew nothing of Railton's circular. He has face enough for almost anything, but hardly for this. There is one damning fact which he cannot shirk. Bailton asks that all contributions shall be made "payable to William Booth, as usual."

Bailton spreads the butter pretty freely on Booth and his family. He says that their devotion to the Army has "loaded them with care, and often made them suffer weakness and pain." As to Mr. Bramwell Booth, in particular, we are informed that he has worked so hard behind the scenes, as Chief of the Staff, that many of his hairs are grey at twenty-seven. Poor Bramwell! The Army should present him with a dozen bottles of hair restorer. Perhaps his young wife will renew his raven head by imitating the lady in the fable, and pulling out all the grey hairs.

In order to compensate this noble family in some degree for their marvellous devotion to the great cause, Bailton proposes that wedding presents in the shape of cash should be made to Mr. Bramwell Booth on the day of his marriage. Whatever money is received will go, not to the young gentleman personally, but to reducing the Army debt of £11,000. But as the Army property is all in Booth's hands, and Mr. Bramwell is his heir and successor, it is obvious that any reduction of the debt will be so much clear gain to the firm.

The General evidently saw that the case was a delicate one; so Bailton sends out a private circular, which he excuses on the ground that "any public appeal would not be at all agreeable to Mr. Bramwell's own feelings." Of course not. But we dare say the wedding presents will be agreeable enough. As this is a strong point with the firm, Bailton repeats it later on. "I do not wish," he says, "to make any public announcement of this." The reason of this secrecy is doubtless the same as that which prompts the General to exclude reporters and interlopers from his all-night meetings. Only the initiated are allowed in, and they of course may be safely trusted.

With the circular Bailton sent out envelopes in which the pious dupes were to forward their contributions; and printed slips, headed "Wedding Presents to Mr. Bramwell Booth," on which they were asked to specify the amount of their gift and the sin from which the Salvation Army had rescued them. This printed slip contains a list of sins, which would do credit to a Jesuit confessor. Booth has we think missed his vocation. He might have achieved real distinction in the army of Ignatius Loyola.

The circular is a wonderful mixture of piety and business. Nearly every sentence contains a little of both. The cash will not only gladden the hearts of the Booths, but "make the devil tremble," and "give earth and hell another shock." This last bit of extravagance is rather puzzling. That hell should receive another shock is very proper, but why is there to be an earthquake at the same time?

We have said enough to show the true character of this cadging trick. It throws a strong light on the business methods of this pious showman. Booth is playing a very astute game. By reducing the Army to military discipline, and constituting himself its General, he retains an absolute command over its resources, and is able to crush out all opposition and silence all criticism. He wields a more than Papal despotism. All the higher posts are held by members of his own family. His eldest son is appointed as his successor. The property thus remains in the family, and the Booth dynasty is established on a solid foundation. Such an impudent imposture would scarcely be credible if it were not patent that there is still amongst us a vast multitude of two-legged sheep, who are ready to follow any plausible shepherd, and to yield up their fleeces to his shears.

www.ingramcontent.com/pod-product-compliance
Lightning Source LLC
Chambersburg PA
CBHW011255040426
42453CB00015B/2418